American College Personnel Association

The American College Personnel Association (ACPA) is one of the largest and most comprehensive national associations for student affairs administrators, faculty, and graduate students. Established in 1924, ACPA has 6,500 individual members and 450 institutionally based memberships. ACPA's overall mission is to serve college and university student affairs educators by providing professional development programs, scholarly publications, government relations information, internship opportunities, and principles of best practice in student affairs to enhance educators' effectiveness in and commitment to developing students in higher education.

For further information about ACPA membership, benefits, and services, please contact

ACPA
One Dupont Circle, N.W., Suite 300
National Center for Higher Education
Washington, D.C. 20036-1110
Telephone: (202) 835-2272
Fax: (202) 296-3286
E-mail: info@acpa.nche.edu
Website: www.acpa.nche.edu

National Association of Student Personnel Administrators

The National Association of Student Personnel Administrators (NASPA) is a leading voice for student affairs administration, policy, and practice. It addresses critical issues in student affairs and seeks to enrich the educational experience for all college and university students. As a national association, NASPA promotes leadership in higher education, advocates for students, and provides cutting-edge tools and programs to higher education practitioners. Since 1918, student affairs administrators have turned to NASPA as the premier resource for high-quality programs and information on current issues affecting campus policies and students' needs. NASPA's mission is to serve students, student affairs administrators, faculty, and other professionals who are actively involved in facilitating student learning in higher education.

For additional information on NASPA or its membership, publications, or professional development programs, visit the NASPA website at www.naspa.org or contact the national office at

NASPA
1875 Connecticut Avenue, N.W.
Suite 418
Washington, D.C. 20009-5728
Telephone: (202) 265-7500
Fax: (202) 797-1157
E-mail: office@naspa.org

Good Practice in Student Affairs

Gregory S. Blimling
Elizabeth J. Whitt
and Associates

Good Practice in Student Affairs

Principles to Foster
Student Learning

Jossey-Bass Publishers
San Francisco

Published in association with the American College Personnel Association and the National Association of Student Personnel Administrators.

Jossey-Bass books and products are available through most bookstores. To contact Jossey-Bass directly, call (888) 378-2537, fax to (800) 605-2665, or visit our website at www.josseybass.com.

Substantial discounts on bulk quantities of Jossey-Bass books are available to corporations, professional associations, and other organizations. For details and discount information, contact the special sales department at Jossey-Bass.

TCF Manufactured in the United States of America on Lyons Falls Turin Book. This paper is acid-free and 100 percent totally chlorine-free.

Library of Congress Cataloging-in-Publication Data

Good practice in student affairs: principles to foster student
learning / Gregory S. Blimling, Elizabeth J. Whitt and associates.
    p. cm.
  Includes bibliographical references and index.
  ISBN 0-7879-4457-2
  1. Student affairs services—United States.   2. College
students—United States.   3. Academic achievement—United States.
I. Blimling, Gregory S.   II. Whitt, Elizabeth J.
  LB2342.9 .G66 1999
  378.1'94—dc21

                                                   99-6119

FIRST EDITION
HB Printing   10 9 8 7 6 5 4 3 2 1

The Jossey-Bass
Higher and Adult Education Series

Contents

Preface

In 1996, we recommended to Paul Oliaro, president of the American College Personnel Association (ACPA), and to Suzanne Gordon, president of the National Association of Student Personnel Administrators (NASPA), that the two organizations sponsor the development of principles of good practice for student affairs. The associations agreed and appointed a study group to draft the principles in time for the 1997 joint convention in Chicago. The eleven members of the group were Gregory Blimling (Appalachian State University, co-chairperson), Elizabeth Whitt (University of Iowa, co-chairperson), Marcia Baxter Magolda (Miami University), Arthur Chickering (Vermont College, Norwich University), Johnetta Cross-Brazzell (Spelman College), Jon Dalton (Florida State University), George Kuh (Indiana University), Ernest Pascarella (University of Iowa), Linda Reisser (Suffolk County Community College, now at Portland Community College), Larry Roper (Oregon State University), and Charles Schroeder (University of Missouri-Columbia).

Selected to represent different types of institutions, study group members were also chosen on the basis of their knowledge and contributions to student affairs research and student affairs professional organizations. We wanted people who were good thinkers who had the experience and knowledge to help sort through the many issues that had to be debated to arrive at a common set of principles for the practice of student affairs.

In July 1996, the study group met for three days in Chicago. Prior to the meeting, study group members read a set of higher education reports, research studies, and other documents relevant to a discussion of principles for student affairs. The principles were to be designed to extend the foundations of student affairs work as stated in *The Student Personnel Point of View* (American Council on Education, 1937) and other documents such as those developed by the Tomorrow's Higher Education (Brown, 1972) project, *A Perspective on Student Affairs* (National Association of Student Personnel Administrators, 1987), *Reasonable Expectations* (Kuh, Lyons, Miller, and Trow, 1994), and *The Student Learning Imperative* (American College Personnel Association, 1994). In addition, the principles of good practice were to be grounded in the most current research and thinking in the field as well as an understanding of the issues of external and internal context, such as emphases on undergraduate learning and institutional accountability, that called for a shift in the practice and philosophy of student affairs work.

Consensus-building rarely is easy, and each idea was debated, researched, and discussed many times. More than twelve drafts of the principles were circulated to members of the study group, and at least three versions were distributed to the leadership of NASPA and ACPA. Drafts of the principles also were introduced at regional student affairs meetings for input; several of these versions were discussed in graduate preparation programs in student affairs.

Some of the feedback suggested that the principles should be arranged in some kind of order. Although we had discussed the possibility of ranking or ordering the principles, no particular order was apparent to everyone. After some discussion, and based on suggestions we received from others, we decided to arrange the principles according to involvement with students and reflection of core values of student affairs. We decided, for example, that a commitment to active learning best represented the central purpose of student affairs work, so that principle would be listed first. Other principles followed from this student learning focus. Although the principles are ordered in this fashion, they are not meant to be hierarchical; one principle is not necessarily more important than the others.

After almost a year of discussion, feedback, and revision, we reached consensus on a set of principles we were ready to share with the ACPA and NASPA memberships at the joint ACPA/NASPA convention in Chicago in 1997. That draft of *Principles of Good Practice for Student Affairs* was distributed to the approximately 8,000 convention participants, and four open forums and one general session at the convention were devoted to soliciting wide-ranging and in-depth feedback about the principles. In more than twelve hours of discussion about the principles at the convention, we learned that there was overwhelming support for them. Most of the feedback we received focused on the impetus for developing the principles and sought suggestions about how they might be used by student affairs practitioners. As you might expect, we also received many suggestions for clarification of language and wording, and there were a few questions about aspects of student affairs work that were not specifically addressed by the principles. Nevertheless, we left the convention with the seven principles intact.

The feedback received at the 1997 ACPA/NASPA convention was incorporated into several subsequent drafts of the *Principles* document. During the development of the principles, a simultaneous discussion ensued about developing some means to operationalize the principles in a form similar to the instruments that were developed from the *Principles of Good Practice for Undergraduate Education* (Chickering and Gamson, 1987). A separate committee headed by ACPA President Paul Oliaro and former NASPA President Suzanne Gordon worked with a group of volunteers to develop an inventory of items relevant to the principles identified by the study group. The *Principles of Good Practice*, including the inventory, was published in March 1998 as a joint ACPA/NASPA statement, the first joint statement from those two organizations in many years.

Principles of Good Practice was written to help build general agreement about actions associated with high-quality learning experiences for undergraduate students. It defines a common agenda for student affairs work that supplements, rather than replaces, the previous works of ACPA and NASPA. What the *Principles* document did not do was fully explain each of the principles, the research on which it was based, the rationale for inclusion, and illustrations of their use. This book was written by the study group members to accomplish those goals.

March 1999   Gregory S. Blimling
                                                Boone, North Carolina

                                                Elizabeth J. Whitt
                                                Iowa City, Iowa

The Authors

Gregory S. Blimling is Vice Chancellor for Student Development and Professor of Human Development and Psychological Counseling at Appalachian State University in North Carolina. He is editor of the *Journal of College Student Development* and is a Senior Scholar of ACPA. Awards for his work in student affairs include the Elizabeth Greenleaf Distinguished Alumni Award from Indiana University, the Melvene Hardee Award for Achievement in Student Personnel Work, the NASPA Melvene Hardee Dissertation of the Year Award, and the Bowling Green State University Special Achievement Award.

Johnetta Cross Brazzell is Vice President for Student Affairs and Professor at the University of Arkansas. She was formerly Vice President for Student Affairs and Professor at Spelman College. Her research interests include the history of higher education, black colleges, and diversification of postsecondary education.

Jon C. Dalton is Vice President for Student Affairs and Associate Professor of Higher Education at Florida State University. He has served as president of the National Association of Student Personnel Administrators (NASPA) and directs the annual Institute on College Student Values held at Florida State University.

George D. Kuh is Professor of Higher Education and Associate Dean of the Faculties at Indiana University-Bloomington, where he also directs the College Student Experiences Questionnaire and Distribution Program. He is past president of the Association for the Study of Higher Education (ASHE). His research and scholarly activities focus on campus cultures, out-of-class experiences of undergraduates, and the institutional conditions that foster student learning.

Marcia B. Baxter Magolda is Professor of Educational Leadership at Miami University. She teaches student development theory and inquiry courses in the college student personnel master's program. Her scholarship addresses the evolution of epistemological development in college and young adult life, the role of gender in development, and pedagogy to promote epistemological development. Her books include *Knowing and Reasoning in College* (Jossey-Bass, 1992). She serves on the editorial board of the *Review of Higher Education*, the Board of Contributors of *About Campus*, and is a member of the ACPA Senior Scholars.

Ernest T. Pascarella is the Mary Louise Petersen Professor of Higher Education at the University of Iowa. His research interests focus on the impact of college on students. He is the author (with Patrick Terenzini) of the 1991 Jossey-Bass book, *How College Affects Students*, which received the 1991 Research Achievement Award from ASHE. Pascarella has also received a number of other national awards for his research. These include the 1987 Sidney Suslow Award from the Association for Institutional Research, the 1988 Outstanding Contribution to Research Award from NASPA, the 1989 Distinguished Research Award from Division J of AERA, and the 1992 Contribution to Knowledge Award from the ACPA.

Linda Reisser is Dean of Students at Portland Community College in Portland, Oregon. Previously she served as Dean of Students at

Suffolk County Community College's Ammerman Campus in Selden, New York. She also served as a student affairs dean at Rockland Community College in Suffern, New York, Whatcom Community College in Bellingham, Washington, and South Dakota State University in Brookings, South Dakota. Reisser is coauthor of the revised version of *Education and Identity*, with Arthur W. Chickering.

Larry D. Roper has served as Vice Provost for Student Affairs and Professor of Ethnic Studies at Oregon State University since 1995. He has held numerous positions in student affairs, including Director of Housing, Associate Dean of Students, Coordinator of Minority Affairs, and Vice President for Student Affairs/Dean of Students. Publications and presentations reflect interests and experiences in topics such as individual and institutional racism in education and society, institutional diversity efforts, college athletics, leadership development, community development, and student development.

Charles C. Schroeder is Vice Chancellor for Student Affairs at the University of Missouri-Columbia. He previously served as the chief student affairs officer at Mercer University, Saint Louis University, and the Georgia Institute of Technology. He has assumed various leadership roles in ACPA, including two terms as president in 1986 and 1993. He was recognized by ACPA for his contributions to higher education by being honored as the recipient of the Esther Lloyd-Jones Professional Service Award. He was also named a Senior Scholar of the association. He is the co-executive editor of *About Campus*, published bimonthly by Jossey-Bass. He was instrumental in creating the document, "The Student Learning Imperative: Implications for Student Affairs" (SLI).

Elizabeth J. Whitt is an associate professor in the College of Education at the University of Iowa and coordinator of the Student

Development in Postsecondary Education program. She worked in residence life and student affairs administration at Michigan State, University of Nebraska-Lincoln, and Doane College (NE). She serves on the editorial board of the *Journal of College Student Development* and is associate editor of the *New Directions for Student Services* monograph series. Whitt received the Early Career Scholar Award from ASHE in 1995.

Identifying the Principles That Guide Student Affairs Practice

Gregory S. Blimling and Elizabeth J. Whitt

In recent years, American higher education has faced the uncertainties of constant change amid crises of confidence and external criticism (National Association of State Universities and Land-Grant Colleges [NASULGC], 1997; The Boyer Commission on Educating Undergraduates in the Research University [Boyer Commission], 1998; Wingspread Group, 1993a). Much of the criticism has focused on higher education's failure to engage students actively in the teaching and learning enterprise. As a consequence, a flurry of reform reports such as *Returning to Our Roots: The Student Experience*, by the Kellogg Commission (NASULGC, 1997), and *Reinventing Undergraduate Education: A Blueprint for America's Research Universities* (Boyer Commission, 1998) have recommended that colleges and universities focus attention and resources on making undergraduate students and their learning the first priority.

In this chapter we explore some of the forces influencing change in student affairs, advance a philosophy of student-centered education consistent with the heritage of student affairs, and identify some fundamental assumptions that sustain this philosophy. We conclude with an examination of *Principles of Good Practice for Student Affairs* (American College Personnel Association and National Association of Student Personnel Administrators, 1997) and discuss how that document can help student affairs professionals make student learning their first priority. This overview serves as an introduction to seven of the eight chapters that follow, each of which expands on one of the principles of good practice in student affairs.

Forces of Change

We who work in higher education are confronted regularly by lists of challenges we face as the year 2000 approaches. A recent example came from the NASULGC report, mentioned earlier, *Returning to Our Roots: The Student Experience*. According to the university presidents who were its authors, "we are beset by challenges" (NASULGC, 1997, p. 1), including increasing (and increasingly diverse) enrollments, increasing competition, declining funding and public trust, and increasing pressure for accountability for achieving desired outcomes. Closer to home, the senior scholars of the American College Personnel Association (1998) described eight trends influencing the future of student affairs: (1) student access to higher education, (2) technology, (3) collaborations and partnerships with faculty, (4) accountability, (5) affordability, (6) new teaching and learning strategies, (7) changing faculty, staff, and student roles, and (8) changing governmental roles. For the purposes of this chapter, we have identified five challenges—or, as we describe them, forces of change—that have particular implications for the work of student affairs administrators: (1) a changing student population, (2) electronic educational technologies, (3) accountability for outcomes, (4) affordability of higher education, and (5) changing faculty, staff, and student roles.

A Changing Student Population

Among the forces altering higher education is a changing student population. Nearly 65 percent of all high school graduates matriculate into a postsecondary institution. Between 1964 and 1994, the percentage of students of color in postsecondary institutions increased from about 7 percent to about 25 percent (National Center for Education Statistics [NCES], 1994; Pascarella and Terenzini, 1998). Growth in minority enrollments has been particularly strong since the early 1980s. Between 1984 and 1994, colleges and universities experienced a 61 percent increase in Asian, African-American, Hispanic, and Native American students (Pascarella and Terenzini, 1998). During the same time period, the number of white undergraduates rose by only 5.1 percent (Pascarella and Terenzini, 1998).

As of the late 1980s, women were more than half (55 percent) of the undergraduate population (Astin, 1993, 1998; Levine and Cureton, 1998a, 1998b; Shavlik, Touchton, and Pearson, 1989). In addition, by the mid-1990s, about 44 percent of all undergraduates were more than twenty-five years old, about half had jobs in addition to being students, and about 40 percent attended college part-time (Astin, 1993, 1998; Levine and Cureton, 1998a, 1998b; NCES, 1994; Pascarella and Terenzini, 1998). The "traditional" college student—single, white, between the ages of eighteen and twenty-three, attending a four-year residential college full-time, and living on campus—thus constitutes less than 20 percent of today's undergraduates (Levine and Cureton, 1998a, 1998b). Finally, between 1996 and 2005, a 20 percent growth in high school graduates is expected. It is reasonable to expect that the "Tidal Wave II" will be as diverse as today's students and that older students, in particular, will be coming to college in even greater numbers.

Students at different stages of their life experience the university in different ways. Traditional-age college students consume more student affairs resources, and tend to be immersed in more of the issues that student affairs educators have been trained to handle, than older students. Older students are less likely to be interested in joining clubs and organizations or in having the university provide social activities for them. Instead, they are likely to be focused on obtaining the degree that would lead them to career advancement and a better life (Levine and Cureton, 1998). A continuing increase in numbers of older students should therefore encourage student affairs educators to consider how different types of students influence their programs, policies, and services, and how resources should be shifted to accommodate changing demographic profiles of students within a particular institution.

Changes in the student population also are influenced by who has access to higher education. Recent changes in affirmative action programs pose a threat to expanding—or even maintaining—access to higher education for students of color. Although the overall effect of the elimination of affirmative action programs is not yet clear, the early indications appear to be that it will hurt the admission of students of color, especially in professional programs such as law and medicine.

Because higher education is the doorway to many career opportunities and to social advancement, however, ensuring access to higher education is imperative for underrepresented groups in our society. An increasingly diverse student body challenges colleges and, we would argue, student affairs professionals in particular, to provide all students with the assistance and opportunities they need to achieve their educational goals. Today's students bring to campus a broad range of personal, economic, cultural, social, community, and political issues that must be addressed if they are to learn effectively (Astin, 1998; London, 1996; Newton, 1998; Rendon, 1996, 1998; Levine and Cureton, 1998b, 1998c).

Electronic Technologies

Electronic technologies are now a pervasive influence in higher education. Keeping up with the rapidly changing state of the art of such technologies while trying to integrate them effectively into all aspects of the higher education enterprise is one of our greatest challenges. Indeed, such technologies challenge our very assumptions about what a college education should be. To appreciate how great a change this is, consider traditional images of teaching and learning in higher education (Jones, Dolence, and Phipps, 1998):

- Students come in person to campus and receive instruction directly from a teacher.

- Student services are included as part of institutional tuition and fees.

- Students start in the fall or spring term and continue in a course for a specified period of time.

- Students become affiliated with a particular institution, and the institution strives to help them graduate from that institution.

- Alumni develop allegiance to a particular institution, and activities and programs at the institution help to strengthen the ties between alumni and the institution.

- Place, time, sequence of courses, terms of admission, length of instruction, and course content are dictated by the institution.

- Learning is assessed by the completion of specific courses at the determination of the institution.

- Degrees and other credentials are awarded by the institution.

- Continuing education, distance learning, and continuing education credits are treated as a revenue-generating auxiliary enterprise by the institution.

Distance education, through use of the Internet and related forms of remote instruction, have provided an alternative to, and competition for, campus-based experiences. Western Governors University is one example of the potential that electronic technologies have for dramatically altering how higher education is provided. Western Governors University is a virtual university—one without a campus. It was created in 1996 and includes support from seventeen governors in the western states and fourteen business partners, including IBM, SUN, AT&T, Cisco, Three-Com, Microsoft, and others. Western Governor's University does not employ teaching faculty, student affairs administrators, or many other people but, rather, has become essentially a broker for Internet and distance-learning courses. It offers courses provided by colleges, universities, and businesses throughout the United States to students anywhere in the world.

Were Western Governors University the extent of this market, it would pose little threat to how our current assumptions about what a college education should "look like." However, Marchese (1998) identified dozens of college and university systems that have entered the distance-learning market. Among these is California Virtual University, which provides more than seven hundred courses in eighty-one public and private institutions, the Colorado Community College System, which offers associate degrees entirely over the Internet, and for-profit higher education programs such as the University of Phoenix, DeVry Institute of Technology, and the Sylvan learning systems.

These changes evoke new images of a college education:

- Students attend classes without ever entering a campus.

- Students design their own learning programs.

- Students enroll concurrently in multiple institutions.

- Students choose, and pay for, only the services they want.

- Courses are offered in modules of learning that promote skill mastery and the acquisition of competencies.

The precise consequences of such changes are difficult to foresee, but we can assume they will be extensive. One of the most troubling potential consequences is the separation of instruction from student services. For many years, student affairs has argued that it is part of the teaching mission of institutions and makes essential contributions to student learning. In addition, because tuition and fees have traditionally supported a variety of student services, it made sense to assess tuition and fees to all students regardless of which services they used. However, this assumption is not valid in cyberspace.

A series of interesting questions are raised about the role of student affairs in distance education. Because student affairs work has traditionally been campus based, little consideration has been given to how student affairs might confront the issue of distance education. Yet most accrediting agencies require that off-campus site locations provide comparable student services. Exactly what these services are and how they are to be delivered are still open to speculation. What appears to be emerging is a dual form of education: Some students—primarily older, part-time, working people who do not have the opportunity to attend a campus for various reasons— are increasingly using distance education methods either to replace or supplement college educational offerings, while campus-based programs cater to graduate students and traditional-aged undergraduates. In this market, what may emerge in student affairs is a similar array of functions whereby basic student services such as academic advising, registration, and financial aid are offered over the Internet to students who are involved in distance education, while campus-based programs remain geared primarily to traditional undergraduates and to on-campus graduate students.

Accountability

Waning confidence in higher education's ability to make a difference in the lives of students and society, as well as its willingness to effectively and efficiently manage itself, has been accompanied by increasing demands, and higher standards, for accountability (Guskin, 1997). Among the "solutions" imposed by state legislators and governing boards are performance measures based on benchmarks or comparisons among similar institutions. This development has been attributed, in part, to higher education's shift in status from a growth industry to a mature industry: "More than 60 percent of all high school graduates is now going on to postsecondary education. This matriculation rate is being viewed in state capitols as sufficient or even as an over-expansion of higher education. . . . Government treats mature industries very differently from growth industries. . . . It asks hard questions about their cost, efficiency, productivity, and effectiveness. . . . It reduces their autonomy, increases their regulation, and demands greater accountability" (Levine, 1997, p. 31).

Although student affairs organizations are not at the center of controversy over accountability in higher education, criticism of the profession is growing. The complaints leveled against student affairs are part of a much larger agenda of reform that has caused greater scrutiny of virtually every element of higher education. Highly public—and highly publicized—incidents such as hate speech, police drug raids at college fraternities, overnight guests in residence halls, hazing, academic dishonesty, gang rape, binge drinking deaths, acquaintance rapes, and riots by crowds of drunk students typically are laid at the doorstep of student affairs. One result of the increased attention to these issues is a perception that universities shelter students from accountability through a system of disciplinary counseling designed to protect institutions from public scrutiny (Bernstein, 1996; Sheehan, 1996). Although people within the academic community deny that they take this approach with their students, many outside the academic community hear and believe these criticisms.

In this environment of accountability and criticism, assessment of student outcomes takes on greater importance than in the past. Unfortunately, the belief that standardized testing is the best way to determine what students have learned in college is widespread. Too much research suggests otherwise. For the public and for legislators, however, standardized testing is the certification and scientific substitute that they have turned to as faith and credibility in higher education have declined.

Affordability

Another area of scrutiny is the rising cost of college, which raises concerns and controversies about the affordability of higher education. As a result of budget constraints in the early 1990s during a period of economic recession and increasing pressure to reorder public support to address Medicare, criminal justice systems, and K–12 education, colleges' and universities' portions of public funding and federal support declined. They responded to these budget constraints with tuition and fee increases. Estimates by the National Commission on the Cost of Higher Education (1998) concluded that between 1988 and 1997, the annual cost at public four-year institutions rose approximately 51 percent and at private institutions by approximately 33 percent. Although figures of this type can be manipulated and costs are not uniform across all institutions, few could dispute that the cost of higher education has increased at a rate significantly higher than that of inflation. Between 1990 and 1998, costs of tuition and fees have increased at an annual rate of between 4 percent and 12 percent (Gose, 1998). Recent public attention to the affordability of higher education has had a somewhat "chilling" influence on discussions among trustees and others about further increases in tuition.

Such responses to external constraints force institutions to make choices that can disadvantage programs and services outside the classroom. Outsourcing, privatizing, reengineering, and downsizing thus could take on new meanings in student affairs, particularly if student affairs programs and activities are seen as ancillary to the mission of the institution. For example, in his 1994 *Change* article on improving administrative productivity in higher education, Antioch University Chancellor Alan Guskin made the following assertion: "Strategically, enhancing student learning and reducing student costs are, in my judgment, the primary yardstick [for organizational effectiveness]. *Since the faculty and academic areas are most directly tied to student learning, alterations in the lower priority support areas must precede* [major changes in the role of the faculty] [emphasis added]" (1994a, p. 29).

The best predictor of future behavior is probably past behavior. And in the past when economic cuts have hit higher education, student affairs has taken its proportional share but usually not more than its portion (Dungee, 1996). As long as higher education continues to move in the way that it has in the past, student affairs can be asked to shoulder its share of the burden of cost cuts. However, if student affairs programs and activities are seen as ancillary to the mission of the institution, possibly done better by companies offering service sector management, and financial analysis shows considerable comparative cost advantages to the institution, student affairs may be dramatically altered on those college campuses.

The problem is not change. The problem is that once change happens, it becomes very difficult to recapture what was lost. When an institution outsources its food service, few have the management skill and financial depth subsequently to construct their own campus food service even when they are dissatisfied with the contract food service. The usual method is to find a different contractor in the hope that a different company will provide better service. Health services, counseling centers, and maintenance programs that have been outsourced have faced similar problems. Once the service is taken out of the university's supervision and turned over to a contractor, it is very difficult to reconstruct what has been lost, even when it is the best decision for the institution.

Changing Faculty, Staff, and Student Roles

Institutions of higher education are becoming more complex, and with that complexity have come a loss in the sense of community and a type of collective disassociation. Students are one of the primary losers in the fragmented educational process presented on many college campuses.

Frequently absent in institutions is a coordinated effort in which the student is the center of learning. Instead, learning can be piecemeal, directed by the student, with varying degrees of quality experience. A student graduating from an institutional experience such as this may have part of his or her education taken over the Internet, part taken at a community college and transferred to the institution, part taken part-time at night or just on the weekends, and part taken through correspondence courses or through a travel-abroad program.

Making analogies between higher education and business is always problematic. But if we were to draw an analogy, it would be like assembling an automobile from various parts gathered in various locations without any person directly supervising the process and without any quality control. The presumption is that all parts are equal and when assembled they will work and create a functioning machine with performance equal to one that has been assembled by a group of craftsmen working collaboratively toward a common end.

All of this transition both with students and at institutions presents another problem. Change seems to be accelerating, and with it the complexity of college life, changing at a pace that makes work more difficult. Stress and burnout among faculty and administrators is common. More interesting is that as the rate of change expands, knowledge expands; and with it comes increasing specialization, more narrowly focused learning, and less interconnectedness, not only between disciplines but within disciplines.

At one time student affairs was a specialty. Today student affairs comprises a variety of specialties. It is difficult to move from a position in career counseling to one in financial aid or to move from being a financial aid administrator to being the director of the student union. Each of these areas has become a separate and relatively distinct specialty within student affairs. Most academic fields are even more specialized. Specialization is a natural outgrowth of any organization and discipline, but it has reached such a magnitude in higher education that we are quickly losing sight of the overarching role of developing an educated citizen.

Fragmentation and compartmentalization in higher education is not new. What is of concern is how this has influenced the education of students. In many cases, it has presented a fragmented, nonlinear developmental education in which students experience at random parts of the university and educational forums. The student is left to assemble these parts into some type of meaningful, coherent whole to form an education. Although there are support services such as academic advising that may be available, the quality of this advising and the ability to have a coherent interconnected program for every individual student varies considerably.

Content-Centered Versus Student-Centered Education

To respond to the challenges posed by these forces of change, higher education reformers and others call for a focus on the primary purpose of higher education (cf., Boyer Commission, 1998; NASULGC, 1997; Wingspread Group, 1993a): undergraduate student learning. Even with agreement about the purpose, there is a difference of opinion about how to achieve that purpose. The two basic approaches can be classified as *content-centered* education and *student-centered* education. Those who hold the *content-centered* view of education see higher education as a means to social mobility and a better life through the mastery of a defined body of knowledge and skills. It is characterized by specialization and professionalization required for performance in industry. The focus is on "training" to meet the needs for an educated work force. In this view, higher education can be delivered in any fashion and, with development of electronic technologies, at almost any location. Credits toward graduation or other certification are gathered from various colleges, universities, and other sources. A licensing or certifying examination might be given to standardize the knowledge necessary to enter employment in the field, and students can be graduated from a university without ever setting foot on the campus or meeting in person with a faculty member or another student.

The contrast to content-centered education is *student-centered* education. Developing an educated citizen is at the heart of this education. Content mastery is important but the body of information to be mastered and the purpose are different. Here the curricular focus is on preparing a liberally educated person who can earn a living and knows how to live. Good citizenship, ethics, values, and an appreciation for the aesthetic qualities of life are accepted as goals in addition to the mastery of information.

Student affairs had its origin in the student-centered philosophy. Throughout the history of the profession, student affairs educators have assumed that higher education environments are organized to assist students with the fulfillment of their full human potential.

The student-centered orientation for higher education is reflected in the shift from viewing colleges as places where instruction takes place to places where learning is fostered. In their description of this shift, Barr and Tagg (1995) noted: "In the Learning Paradigm, a college's purpose is not to transfer knowledge, but to create environments and experiences that bring students to discover and conduct knowledge for themselves, to make students members of communities of learners that make discoveries and solve problems. The college aims, in fact, to create a series of ever more powerful learning environments" (Barr and Tagg, 1995, pp. 14, 15).

If one assumes that the purpose of higher education is not to transfer knowledge but rather to provide learning, then everyone who works with students is engaged in achieving that purpose. If creating "ever more powerful learning environments" and bringing students to the center of a community of learners are aims of college, student affairs professionals play an essential role.

Responding to Change

In a dynamic environment buffeted by sweeping issues of financial, demographic, legal, and political change, strategic planning is all but impossible. Doing more of the same—the most usual response to change—is also unlikely to work during a period of dramatic reform. And suggesting new and untried avenues of intervention in student affairs seems like a risky and unwise adventure in periods of uncertainty and reform.

The approach that we recommend and discuss throughout this book is a student-centered approach based on a set of principles that we have distilled from the best practices in student affairs. This best practices approach has several advantages: (1) it avoids advocating a singular mission for all of student affairs regardless of the institution it serves; (2) it focuses on commonalties among divergent views in student affairs as opposed to legitimate differences about how student affairs programs should be administered; (3) it offers themes that can be easily understood by those inside and outside higher education; and (4) the best practices approach forms principles that can be applied in multiple situations.

From our analysis of higher education in its current state and what the future is likely to hold, we believe that changes are necessary in student affairs, as they are in other parts of higher education. We also believe that the traditions, heritage, and foundations of the field revealed through the research and the founding documents of the profession hold the keys to reshaping student affairs work. We therefore conclude that the principles of good practice offer the guidepost most useful to student affairs in the transformation of higher education. Unlike rigid standards, principles allow application in many varied educational institutions with diverse groups of students and campus cultures. We look next at each of the principles.

Understanding the Seven Principles of Good Practice

The principles of good practice for student affairs are grounded in the traditional belief of the holistic development of students, which is more generally referred to now as a *student learning approach*.

Good Practice in Student Affairs Engages Students in Active Learning

This principle was selected as the first principle because it embodies what student affairs does most and what student affairs' historical mission has been. Graduation rates, student satisfaction, alumni support, critical thinking, interpersonal skills, and functionally transferable skills are either developed or enhanced through activities outside the classroom that involve students in meaningful ways.

Outward Bound education is based on this philosophy. When students go mountain climbing or participate in a survival experience, the goal of the program is generally not the development of specific skill (that is, mountain climbing or high-ropes agility), it is the development of self-knowledge, self-concept, self-esteem, confidence, team building, and other related skills. So it is with most of the activities in which student affairs finds itself engaged. Student affairs is about structuring peer group environments in ways to support the achievement of valued educational goals. We believe that this concept is best expressed by the first principle; that is, to engage students in active learning.

This principle also speaks to the larger issue of student affairs' role in higher education. It states clearly that student affairs organizations are part of the educational mission of higher education, connected directly with the learning experiences of students. Out-of-class learning experiences are not ancillary to a liberal education but are central to it.

Good Practice in Student Affairs Helps Students Develop Coherent Values and Ethical Standards

One of the most consistent criticisms of higher education in general, and student affairs specifically, has been the lack of attention paid to the development of students' ethics and values. In part, this criticism stems from a rise in public concern about drunkenness, drug abuse, violence toward women, suicides, academic dishonesty, and sexual promiscuity among college students. Unfortunately, higher education has in recent years neglected its historic commitment to building character, values, and a commitment to responsible citizenship. The fruits of this neglect are evident.

Cultivating character and intellect is the bedrock of American higher education. Accomplishing these objectives has traditionally involved education in a community that articulates its values and creates an environment that nurtures these values in students. Although higher education has a responsibility both historically and educationally for developing in students values and ethical principles, exactly what those values should be and which ethical principles is a decision that institutions must decide based on their mission and constituency.

Little of this comes as a surprise to student affairs educators who have for years promoted issues of student responsibility under codes of student conduct and academic integrity. Most institutions have worked diligently to ensure that their students acquire these skills. Therefore, in adding this principle, we have done nothing more than advance what has already been a historic commitment of student affairs to the development of education and values in students. However, this principle suggests that this same commitment to students' values and ethics must occupy a larger role in the decision, policies, and practices influenced by student affairs.

Good Practice in Student Affairs Sets and Communicates High Expectations for Learning

Setting high expectations is a proven method for instruction in higher education and is one of the tools that student affairs administrators need to have available to help students progress in education. It may be that the expectations they help students set for themselves involve assuming leadership positions, achieving high academic performance on standardized exams or in particular courses, completing more than one bachelor's degree in four years, mastering a language prior to a foreign exchange program, traveling abroad, becoming a resident assistant, or becoming the president of the student body.

One way that universities set high expectations for students is by trusting them and giving them responsibility. At Appalachian State University, certain supervisory positions with a high degree of responsibility are intentionally reserved for students who have the skills and potential to do these activities. In many cases it would be easier to hire professional staff to perform certain functions and by doing so gain greater continuity between academic years, but important learning opportunities would be denied students. The expectation for the supervisory role in areas such as intramural activities, student union activities, and residence life are clearly delineated to students. They know as they work in other capacities that supervisors are selected based on performance criteria and that their performance is judged on a regular basis to determine their capabilities of moving ahead. Feedback and evaluations are part of the process, and goal setting helps define these expectations.

Good Practice in Student Affairs Uses Systematic Inquiry to Improve Student and Institutional Performance

If you want to know what students think, ask them. Or if you want to know how much students learn, test them. Despite these rather obvious statements, surprisingly few institutions actively engage in either form of outcome assessment. It is difficult to manage what you cannot measure. If student affairs is in the business of student learning, it should be engaged in trying to measure what contributes positively to that process and what interferes with it. Too often, decisions about higher education are made on anecdotal information or on the basis of issues raised by a particular student group. This type of administration is fraught with problems, not the least of which is that often the groups that yell the loudest command the greatest degree of attention.

Higher education administration is an environment in which data are used to make decisions. Student affairs divisions without access to this kind of information are left at a disadvantage in explaining what and how they contribute to the education of students.

Good Practice in Student Affairs Uses Resources Effectively to Achieve Institutional Missions and Goals

On most college campuses, a sizable portion of the auxiliary services rests in the division of student affairs. Housing, food services, health services, and many other auxiliary enterprises of the institution are fee-based and require the effective allocation of resources to achieve the institutional missions. A principle of good practice in student affairs, as it is in other forms of higher education, is the responsible stewardship of students' money. Student affairs educators must know how to manage resources to get the most from them.

Good Practice in Student Affairs Forges Educational Partnerships That Advance Student Learning

Collaboration has been a recurring theme in student affairs' history. Unfortunately, it is usually easier to write about what should be done than actually do it. In an ideal world, university vice presidents would not engage in power struggles or argue over resources, and they would share a common philosophy and champion each other on every occasion. Many colleges function around territories of responsibilities and expertise. Stray too far outside of your specialty and you are likely to enter into the territory of another. Depending on the level of intrusion, a conflict may arise over even the most trivial issues.

Collaboration does not come easily or naturally owing to the personalities, history, expertise, and territories that define colleges and universities. What is more remarkable is that collaboration does occur. What makes it possible is a common desire to do good for students. Few serve in a university who do not care about students. Although there are times when some may wish to shut their door to the onslaught of some students who can challenge one's strongest urges of civility, ultimately it is this unifying issue that defines the university community and opens the door to collaboration.

Even in this environment, where there are specialties, territories, and defined areas of responsibility, partnerships and collaborative projects happen with frequency. They are seen in committee assignments, in joint ventures such as homecoming, family weekend, and university strategic planning. Admissions committees, crisis intervention teams, disciplinary committees, and a host of other issues on the campus tend to be collective decisions of the university community.

Most important, student affairs needs to be involved in the partnership relationship with academic affairs in advancing student learning. Student affairs needs to champion the cause of academic affairs and, in so doing, join and contribute to the process. Student affairs' viability is strengthened when the focus of discussion is the student and what he or she learns. Although faculty may not truly understand or appreciate many of the contributions of student affairs educators, they do understand and appreciate the interconnectedness of the educational experiences, particularly the partnerships that are formed together toward a common end that both wish to achieve.

Good Practice in Student Affairs Builds Supportive and Inclusive Communities

American higher education has been built on the Jeffersonian ideal of equality, democracy, social betterment, universal literacy, and education for all. Although it has taken years to increase access to higher education, the greatest challenge is now to make educational environments accepting of the diverse group of students who wish to take advantage of what they have to offer.

Developing a sense of community in a highly diverse institution comprising many specialties and dramatically different forms of interaction is not an easy task. Smaller, private, particularly religiously affiliated, colleges usually have a much easier time of defining exactly what they mean by community and exactly how they hope to fulfill it. More complex institutions struggle with the issue but use the term with the same degree of commitment. Regardless of how institutions are organized, how complex or how simple they may appear to those within and outside the institution, they all strive to achieve a sense of community and acceptance by all of its members.

Building community is an essential element in building the support network necessary for students' success and achievement. Student affairs' role includes working with students to help them achieve a sense of belonging and to build a sense of community and support among students, allegiance to the institution, and commitment to one another.

Concluding Thoughts

Principles of Good Practice for Student Affairs demonstrates and reinforces the field's commitment to student learning and institutional effectiveness. Grounded in compelling research on college students and a wealth of practical experience in student affairs work, the principles are intended to help create learning-oriented student affairs divisions. The chapters that follow provide research, examples, and uses for the principles that we believe best guide the practice of student affairs work.

2

Engaging Students in Active Learning

Marcia B. Baxter Magolda

Active learning invites students to bring their life experiences into the
learning process, reflect on their own and others' perspectives as
they expand their viewpoints, and apply new understandings to their
own lives. Good student affairs practice provides students with opportunities for experimentation through programs focused on engaging students in various learning experiences. These opportunities
include experiential learning such as student government, collective
decision making on educational issues, field-based learning such as
internships, peer instruction, and structured group experiences such
as community service, international study, and resident advising
[ACPA and NASPA, 1997, p. 3].

Active learning draws learners into the process of learning and
encourages them to become authors of their own perspectives.
Arthur Chickering and Zelda Gamson (1987b) emphasized this connection between self and learning in one of their "Seven Principles
for Good Practice in Undergraduate Education": "[Students must]
talk about what they are learning, write about it, relate it to past experiences, and apply it to their daily lives. They must make what
they learn part of themselves" (p. 1). Parker Palmer offered a similar description in defining the goals of good teaching: "to draw students into the process, the community, of knowing" (1990, p. 12).

Jim, a participant in a study of college students' learning (Baxter Magolda, 1992), described the influence of active learning on

his college experience. Reflecting on college one year after graduation, he said:

> I think the general theme of what I got out of my college
> career was a chance to work with a lot of different peo-
> ple and to see so many different perspectives on life
> through my male-female relationships, my fraternity
> brotherhood relationships, through my acquaintance re-
> lationships. I look back at college and I say 'Wow! That
> was great.' A lot of it was the interaction with people
> and a chance to see things in different ways and really
> grow as a person. You'd take up issues like abortion and
> how your opinions have evolved on that throughout the
> college years. And dealing with women. When I first
> came into college it was like the woman should be the
> subordinate type person. Now from my involvement
> with people in school I've gotten away from that where
> it's more of an equal type position. . . . A lot of it was dic-
> tated by environments I was in—student government,
> being a Resident Advisor my sophomore year, campaign
> manager for two years, student credit union, the Na-
> tional College Student Credit Council, my fraternity—
> dealing with people, taking on leadership roles. It's more
> the personal contacts I had with different people.

Jim's story about his cocurricular involvement exemplifies four
characteristics central to the principle of engaging students in active learning. First, Jim brought his life experiences to learning, in
this case to his interactions with his peers. Second, he had opportunities to compare his views to others', opportunities that helped
him reflect on his initial views and alter his beliefs. Third, as Jim
encountered diverse views, he decided which ones to adopt as his
own and which to discard, thereby constructing new and broader
understandings for himself. Finally, he applied these new under-

standings to his life in campus leadership positions and in interpersonal relationships.

Jim's experience matches what most educators hope a college education will accomplish. For example, the Association of American Colleges defines the challenge of college as "empowering individuals to know that the world is far more complex than it first appears, and that they must make interpretive arguments and decisions—judgments that entail real consequences for which they must take responsibility and from which they may not flee by disclaiming expertise" (1991, p. 16).

To make effective arguments, decisions, and judgments, a student must reflect on her own and others' views and integrate them into informed perspectives and understandings. Acknowledging and being accountable for her judgments requires applying these understandings in daily life. Applying new perspectives and understandings, in turn, requires opportunities for active learning.

Making colleges and universities places of active learning is a major undertaking, however. Making room for genuine reflection, integration, and application means loosening controls, encouraging risk taking, and expecting mistakes (Kegan, 1993). If learning is our focus, finding ways to transform our expectations about everyday life on campus is necessary. In this chapter I synthesize the research on active learning and its promise for promoting learning for all students in undergraduate education in the twenty-first century. I then describe successful implementation of this active learning principle in various student affairs contexts. I close the chapter with a discussion about the implications of this principle for our thinking about learning, education, students, and student affairs practice.

The Nature of Active Learning

Active learning has been defined by psychologists, philosophers, and educators in many different ways. I attempt to describe its nature here in a framework applicable to student affairs. Within that framework, however, I introduce perspectives of those who have written extensively on learning, for three reasons. First, implementing active learning requires understanding its intricacies—it is less a matter of technique and more a matter of thinking differently about learning. Second, in the process of teaching students to make effective judgments, less well-informed judgments might occur that bother campus administrators. Student affairs educators who engage in the risks involved in active learning must be able to explain and justify their practices to those who would argue for controlling students rather than facing the ambiguities associated with active learning. Third, faculty are engaged in a national conversation about active learning and student affairs' participation, and the success of that dialogue hinges on being familiar with the learning and teaching perspectives under discussion.

A Bridge Metaphor

Robert Kegan (1994) offered a bridge metaphor for linking students' understanding of themselves and the world around them to educators' goals. He depicted what students understand and how they understand it as one end of a bridge. Educators' goals for what and how students should understand are the other end of the bridge. Kegan admonished, "We cannot simply stand on our favored side of the bridge and worry or fume about the many who have not yet passed over. A bridge must be well anchored on both sides, with as much respect for where it begins as for where it ends" (p. 62).

The task for educators is to know and respect where the bridge begins and help students take the journey to the other side. For example, if we desire students to make informed judgments for which they take responsibility, we must respect that younger students still rely on others to decide what to believe and therefore do not see themselves as responsible. To help students achieve the goal of informed judgment, a bridge must be built from where they are to the skills, attitudes, and behaviors that constitute informed judgment—a bridge that is paved with opportunities for reflection, integration, and application through active learning.

Understanding Students' Side of the Bridge

Students' understanding of themselves and the world around them involves two primary components: the content (what) they understand and the process (or how) by which they understand it. Educators' goals, such as informed judgment, usually require changes in both components. For example, students have some understanding of how alcohol affects the body and the laws on alcohol use. Yet they might believe alcohol will not affect *their* body or that *they* will get caught drinking if they are underage. Changes in the content of their thinking come only from active learning. John Dewey (1916) advanced this notion, describing thinking as the discovery of connections between actions and their consequences. He believed that learning should be an active process in which students rely on their own experiences and available data from others to work through a problem and to generate inferences and tentative explanations. Students then should be given opportunities to further develop their ideas and test them to determine their value. Therefore the components of active learning—experience, reflection, integration, and application—were central to Dewey's view of learning. To change students' misconceptions about alcohol, student affairs can employ reflection, integration, and application after students' inevitable experimentation. Ways to approach this are provided later in this chapter.

Perhaps even more powerful than *what* students understand is the second component—*how* they understand it. How students understand reflects the organizing principles they use to make meaning of their experience. Research indicates that many college students assume that knowledge is certain in some areas and uncertain in others (Baxter Magolda, 1992; Belenky, Clinchy, Goldberger, and Tarule, 1986; King and Kitchener, 1994; Perry, 1970). They adopt the views of authority figures in the areas they believe are certain and look for other means to find the truth in the uncertain areas. For example, many traditional-age college students and young adults internalize the viewpoints of those close to them to the extent that the external viewpoints become their own (Kegan, 1994). Their identity may be defined by how they think others perceive them and their relationships are based on gaining others' approval. Their intrapersonal and interpersonal structures lead them to be influenced by their peers, which could explain why students who "know better" find themselves drinking past the point of control.

So how do students understand themselves and the world around them? Kegan's bridge metaphor emphasizes listening to students to gain access to their understanding and respecting their current way of making meaning, while inviting them on the journey to new understandings.

Three Principles for Bridge Building

This change to new and more complex understandings only takes place when sufficient support exists to adopt a new way of making meaning. Welcoming students' current understandings and challenging them simultaneously can be a tricky process. Too much challenge can result in students' becoming entrenched in their original stance. Kegan (1994) explained that supporting and respecting students' current understandings yet challenging them to move forward implies active learning—that is, providing opportunities to experiment with new perspectives and behaviors and to integrate them into current ways of thinking and acting. From students in my longitudinal study of young adults' intellectual development, I gleaned three principles to guide this effort (Baxter Magolda, 1992).

The first principle, *situating learning in students' experience,* involves using student experience as the context for learning. This first step in active learning anchors learning on the students' side of the bridge by supporting their current beliefs and ways of thinking. Paulo Freire (1970/1986) called this posing problems in the context of students' lives; Ira Shor (1992) emphasized listening to students' language, feelings, and knowledge to establish a base from which to approach subject matter. In the alcohol example, this principle involves eliciting students' thoughts on, and experiences with, alcohol.

The second principle, *validating students as knowers*, involves validating students' ability to think, although not necessarily validating their ideas. This principle supports students' experiences and current ways of thinking by taking them seriously and by respecting students' ability to reflect on their experiences and consider the ideas of others. Inviting the views of all students into the conversation brings to light multiple perspectives. Returning to the alcohol example, this principle mandates not only hearing the student's story and perspectives, but respecting his stance on the issue and working genuinely to understand it, as well as explaining to him others' points of view.

The third principle, *mutually constructing meaning*, describes a joint effort by educator and learner to develop new perspectives and ways of thinking and to apply these new perspectives and structures to everyday life. In the alcohol example this would involve dialogue about the student's thoughts and feelings about the consequences of his alcohol use for his health, academic success, and relationships, and how dealing with these consequences conflicts with his interest in peer acceptance; exploration of alternatives for achieving all his goals; exploration of ways to think differently about his current choices; and help for the student in making his own judgment about how to respond effectively to his situation. Further discussion might explore effective strategies for implementing his decision.

Ira Shor's (1992) caution about mutual dialogue is important here; he noted that the educator brings her knowledge to the dialogue, but rather than imposing it unilaterally, she introduces it in the context of the students' perspectives. An active learning approach therefore does not advocate letting students decide anything they wish, but rather advocates working jointly with students to put educators' knowledge alongside students' and engaging in genuine exploration of both. This entails trusting that students, when given appropriate opportunities and practice, will move toward making increasingly informed decisions.

Reaching the Other Side

The journey across the bridge is not immediate. Letting go of old ways and replacing them with new ones is hard work, particularly if one is unsure about whether one can be accountable for decisions and judgments. Replacing a structure in one dimension of learning (for example, deciding to make one's own decisions) creates conflict in another dimension (for example, gaining the approval of others). Although the term *learning* often brings to mind cognitive development, Kegan (1994) illustrated that a solid sense of identity (intrapersonal) and complex constructions of the relationship of self and other (interpersonal) also are needed for complex meaning-making. Active learning in light of these perspectives extends beyond activity. Active learning involves integration of experience (external or internal) and reflection in making sense of one's experience in new ways.

Why Is Active Learning Good Student Affairs Practice?

To what extent does student affairs engage students in active learning? Jim's story verifies that opportunities for active learning are inherent in student affairs contexts, particularly the opportunity to bring experiences into learning. However, student affairs has historically taken responsibility for helping students form their identity and healthy relationships with others, assuming cognitive aspects of development are more pertinent to classroom learning. Increasingly educators recognize that the cognitive (how students make meaning, interpret knowledge, decide what to believe), intrapersonal (self-identity), and interpersonal (relationships with others) dimensions of learning are intertwined. For example, a student in an abusive relationship can articulate (in the presence of a student affairs educator) that the relationship is problematic and that she should exit it for her own good, yet her sense of self and need for acceptance draws her back into the relationship as soon as she leaves the office. Using knowledge about development in all three dimensions, student affairs educators can restructure practice to create meaningful opportunities for students to make sense of their identity and their relationship needs.

In addition, for many years student affairs literature has emphasized involvement as a major factor in student learning and a focus on involvement is a mainstay in most student affairs practice. But although student affairs practice has always welcomed student involvement (for example, in student government, clubs, and organizations, leadership roles, living environments), it has not always honored or respected student experiences. Nor, I would argue, has it used student experiences as the foundation for efforts to encourage changes in student behaviors and attitudes. For example, alcohol abuse, racism, and eating disorders often are addressed from the educator's viewpoint: excess drinking is dangerous, bigotry hurts everyone in the human community, health is more important than appearance. Student affairs staff exert considerable and careful efforts to help students make good decisions about these serious issues, yet poor judgments persist. Somehow, those efforts miss their mark and the insights and lessons student affairs staff convey do not become part of the fabric of students' lives. Educators often explain this failure in terms of complex factors beyond administrative or institutional control, such as students' personal and family histories or the overriding culture, rather than in terms of the educators' approaches to the problems.

More effective in encouraging real change is posing the problems from students' perspectives. For instance, under what circumstances does it "makes sense" to starve oneself to feel in control of one's life or to drink oneself literally to death to gain acceptance. Identifying, understanding, and validating student perspectives is a necessary foundation for helping students consider alternatives, but it is only a foundation. Moving from current ways of thinking and behaving toward application and integration of new ways requires active learning. Active engagement with peers and educators to explore alternative perspectives about self and relationships can help expand ways of thinking about both. Helping students synthesize these multiple perspectives, to decide what to believe about themselves and how they relate to others, is essential before students can apply new approaches to their daily lives. If student affairs practice, despite its hands-on nature, "tells" students how to be and how to relate to others (for example, don't be racist, don't abuse alcohol), we will be as ineffective in helping students learn how to make informed judgments as faculty whose teaching deposits knowledge in students' heads and notebooks.

Active learning also is warranted in student affairs practice because it creates inclusive learning environments by inviting the experience of all students to become part of the learning process. Serious consideration of and respect for diverse experiences and perspectives offers all students optimal learning opportunities. In addition, remaking students' perspectives in light of multicultural experiences and applying those understandings to their lives offers new possibilities for understanding themselves and their relationship to those around them.

Both public and private life increasingly demand taking responsibility for oneself and others, changing to keep pace with societal changes, and interacting flexibly in an increasingly diverse society. If college graduates are to manage their affairs and become contributing members of contemporary American society, they must develop the capacity for self-authorship and lifelong learning required in a complex world. Russell Warren noted that "active learning has the potential to revolutionize instruction and stir students' enthusiasm for education" (1997, p. 16). Anyone who has talked with college students knows that education could stand to be revolutionized and students' enthusiasm is ripe for stirring. The cocurriculum is the ideal venue in which to promote the kind of learning and development that today's college graduates will need to succeed in the next century.

Implementing Active Learning

We have defined engaging students in active learning as incorporating their life experience, encouraging their reflection on their own and others' views, integrating multiple perspectives into new understandings, and applying those understandings to their lives. Our task is to make what and how students think center stage, respect that experience, and create learning environments that are meaningful to that experience yet facilitative of remaking it. The three principles just described—situating learning in students' experience, validating students' ability to know, and defining learning as mutually constructing meaning—offer one useful framework for engaging students in active learning. Multiple frameworks are possible as long as they retain student perspectives and experiences at the center and incorporate reflection, integration, and application. Excellent models of implementing the three principles illustrate the particulars of incorporating active learning in student affairs policy and programming. The exemplars that follow highlight active learning in two contexts—establishing community norms and staff training. Exploration of how these models apply to multiple student affairs contexts follows.

The Community Standards Model

The University of Nevada, Las Vegas (UNLV) Community Standards Model brings student experience to the forefront in creating norms for residential living. Recognizing that students experienced the hall living environment as controlling, the UNLV staff developed the Community Standards Model to empower students to create healthy living environments. In doing so they created an effective *process* for establishing living group norms and simultaneously promoting active learning. In this model, students play a central role in creating, implementing, and maintaining community standards—"shared agreements that define mutual expectations for how the community will function on an interpersonal level (that is, how the members will relate to and treat each other)" (Piper, 1996, p. 14). However, the model is, more important, an active learning process. Students receive summer mailings explaining the community standards model. Upon arrival on campus, groups of residents meet to generate standards for their particular living unit. Resident adviser staff facilitate the meetings to develop standards. These begin with acquaintanceship activities, a review of the standards model, and discussions of group participation guidelines. After setting the stage with these activities, brainstorming of possible standards occurs, followed by dialogue around proposed standards. The resident adviser assists the group to achieve consensus on a particular set of standards and guides a discussion about accountability for implementing them. The experience that students bring to the living environment is thus welcomed in forming expectations. At the same time, students are introduced to the need to listen to each other and reflect on the perspectives offered by peers.

Opportunities to incorporate new experience and revise perspectives comes in the second phase of the model. The complex nature of residential living quickly introduces situations that are perceived to violate the initial standards (for example, students have different perspectives on what is too loud, students discover issues they did not anticipate). Piper (1997) wrote: "If phase one represents good intentions, then phase two represents real life, that is, standards alone will not guide everyone's behavior" (p. 23). This reality prompts the group to reconvene to further define standards and accountability issues. Meetings for these purposes can be initiated by any member of the community and are again facilitated by resident advisers. The community moves into problem solving in this phase, engaging in dialogue about the meaning of the standard, whether it was realistic, whether changes need to be made, and clarification on acceptable behavior. Agreements made in these problem-solving dialogues clarify and refine the initial standards and model the evolving nature of learning. The need for agreement promotes reflection on multiple perspectives and revision of perspectives accordingly.

Applying new understandings to one's life occurs in phase three of the model, in which particular individuals are asked to respond to the community's concern about their behavior. Called *accountability meetings*, these sessions focus on communication among community members regarding how individual behavior affects the community. Residents share their concerns with the offending person, explain why the person's behavior is problematic for the community, and engage the person in conversation about the issue. The desired outcome is acceptance of personal responsibility for one's behavior and its subsequent impact on the community. Only when the community is unsuccessful in altering a member's behavior is that person referred to disciplinary proceedings outside the community.

The Community Standards Model intentionally used Baxter Magolda's three principles (described earlier in this chapter) for promoting learning (Piper, 1996). This process clearly situates learning in students' experience. Discussion of standards initially stems from pre-arrival experience and later from actual life in the hall. Students' perspectives—on preferences for living standards and responses to violations—stand at the core of the process. Students are validated as knowers in numerous ways. Their experience is valued in setting standards. Their reactions to general and specific violations of standards are respected. Their ability to make, revise, and implement standards for their own behavior validates their ability to take responsibility. Mutual construction of meaning takes place as students learn to work collaboratively with their peers and the staff to develop meaningful standards. Opportunities to express their opinions, struggle to understand conflicts in perspectives, hear the reactions of peers, and jointly decide how to come to agreement offer rich opportunities to engage in active learning.

The Community Standards Model is based on the constructive-developmental theoretical framework (Piper, 1996) and emphasizes the use of peers in the learning process. Kegan's insight on students defining themselves in the context of relationships is used to advantage in asking students to work through standards with each other. The process is meaningful to how residents understand themselves and their relationships with others, thus respecting their end of the bridge, yet facilitative of forming more complex ways of defining self and others. Students participating in the model reported that "they had learned to appreciate their uniqueness, had become more self-aware, more responsible, more confident, more capable of standing up for what they believed, more willing to state their opinion, more understanding of others, more able to stand up for what they wanted, and more willing to object to activities and actions they felt were wrong" (Piper, 1997, p. 24). Active learning helped students achieve the kind of development needed to interact with diverse others in a complex society. Since implementation of the model, positive changes in the overall living environment have also occurred, including an 80 percent drop in damages and false fire alarms and a 66 percent decrease in judicial hearings (Piper, 1997). This model confirms that engaging students in active learning promotes their development and learning and simultaneously achieves institutional goals for a healthy environment.

Use of the model also emphasizes that student affairs contexts offer fertile ground for learning. Piper (1997) pointed out, however, that it requires new thinking about staff hiring, training, and supervision. Resident adviser selection focuses on "attributes such as self-awareness, critical thinking, openness, and ability to listen—rather than more traditional traits such as assertiveness, confrontation skills, and programming ability" (p. 23). Training and supervision focus on group process skills, problem solving, and facilitation of the phases of the community standards model.

Resident Assistant Institute

"The things I learned, I will be able to apply to my personal life and my life as an RA" (Blystone, Conlon, Kooker, Marriner, and Wigton, 1996, p. 4). This comment from a participant in Miami University's Resident Assistant Institute conveys that staff training can be a place to connect learning to one's life. In an attempt to enhance the training of veteran resident assistants (RAs), members of the Residence Life staff developed an institute format for a component of preservice training. The initial institute consisted of five tracks—civic responsibility and enrichment, leadership exploration, service learning, wilderness leadership expedition, and women's wellness—each emphasizing a set of goals for growth for both the resident assistants and their future residents. The creators of the institute grounded their work in experiential learning and student development principles.

The framework for each track merged Pfeiffer and Jones' (1983) five steps of experiential learning (experiencing, publishing, processing, generalizing, applying) with Baxter Magolda's (1992) three principles for promoting intellectual development (Blystone et al., 1996). Experiencing was emphasized via an intensive two- to three-day trip to a location relevant to the track goal. For example, the civic responsibility and enrichment track involved a trip to the state capitol to interact with civic and community leaders because the goal was to help RAs and their residents become leaders in the campus and local community. This format clearly situated learning in students' experience in a substantive manner. Discussions among the participants during the trip offered opportunities to publish how they made sense of interactions with leaders and visits to civic sites and simultaneously validated students as knowers. Discussions were structured next around processing what had been learned, incorporating different views from all participants' experiences, and generalizing learning to the RA position. Planning-programming and community-building efforts for the year offered an opportunity to apply what was learned to practice. These last three steps of the experiential learning model simultaneously focused on mutually constructing meaning with the RAs. Because participants were veteran RAs, their previous experience in the role was also validated as useful in planning new efforts.

The characteristics of active learning are clearly evident in the Resident Assistant Institute. The substantive nature of the experiential component offers an excellent example of bringing students' lives into the learning process. Each group was immersed in some type of meaningful experience. For example, the wilderness leadership expedition focused on leadership and team building in the context of climbing, hiking, and orienteering. Similarly, the service learning track offered intense interaction with foster children to focus on reciprocal learning and social justice. The women's wellness track used the Wellness Model to structure activities to explore topics such as women's leadership and social constructs of body image. The nature of these experiences, in conjunction with participants' previous experiences with college residence hall issues, offered rich opportunities for reflection on multiple views. The processing, generalizing, and application phases of the experience offered a structure in which participants could make meaning of these topics for themselves and decide how to apply those understandings in their RA role. These phases also helped students access, consider, and respect views different from their own and figure out what to believe about those views. As the quote at the outset of the section indicates, many left the experience with insights to apply to their personal lives as well. Participants in the first year of the RA Institute reported that they acquired new knowledge about how to make their community programming meaningful, gained confidence in their ability to work with others, achieved personal insight and fulfillment, and felt a part of a community as a result of the institute (Blystone et al., 1996).

The overwhelming popularity of the first institute led the Office of Residence Life to offer the institute the following year. Active learning was incorporated into the design phase, involving participants in designing the track in which they registered to participate. Although the topics were identified by the facilitators, they were described as an outline of possibilities to be developed by participants. The importance of personal experience was emphasized in the introductory brochure, which stated: "The RA Institute is an opportunity to cultivate a renewed sense of commitment and to promote the personal development of yourself and your residents"

(Miami University Office of Residence Life and New Student Programs, 1997). Reflection and exploration of multiple perspectives were shared as explicit goals—"You will be challenged to remove yourself from your comfort zone and to explore new concepts and thoughts. . . . You will engage in critical dialogue with fellow RAs and gain a fresh, new perspective from your peers" (Miami University Office of Residence Life, 1997). The goals of each track clearly emphasized applying these new perspectives to one's own life and one's RA work. For example, the track on AIDS: impacting America sought to help RAs actively shape the future of AIDS in society; the diversity and development in the arts track sought to bridge art appreciation with the celebration of diversity. One facilitator of the latter track reported that students explored multiple perspectives through being immersed in the culture of a city, exploring how an architectural tour could help them view the world from different perspectives, discussing readings on the cultural dimensions of art, and sharing their diverse experiences in peer dialogues (R. Alldis, personal communication, September 2, 1997). Stirring students' enthusiasm for exploring diversity, usually a major challenge, was successful here through active learning.

New Models for Active Learning

A substantial portion of student affairs work involves helping students learn how to function and live in groups. Although student organizations have multiple goals, inevitably they serve as a context in which students learn interpersonal skills and develop values regarding interacting with others in a community. The Community Standards Model, though set in a residential context, is easily transferable to other group settings. Imagine a house of fraternity brothers engaging in genuine dialogue and exploring multiple perspectives about enculturation into their organization—a dialogue that would resurface as issues with pledging arose. Imagine a student government creating norms for their work and a system for maintaining them to avoid the apathy that generally sets in as some students become central players and others recede into the background. Imagine a special interest group creating norms that make their interaction meaningful rather than simply serving as an entry on a resume.

Using the Community Standards concept in these contexts not only offers rich opportunities for student learning, but also offers possibilities for solving some of the pressing problems we face with student groups, such as inability to manage conflict and lack of accountability for appropriate group behavior. Providing a structure for and facilitating the process of developing community norms in these contexts may be more important emphases for student affairs educators than simply advising groups on activities or policymaking. Just as the Community Standards Model helped students learn to work effectively with others and manage varying interests, using similar processes in student groups would help students learn the skills they will need to work effectively with others in their workplaces, communities, and homes. Perhaps what student groups do (for example, publish a newspaper or plan events) is less important than their learning how to work in a collective.

Community norms are beneficial in groups that convene on a temporary basis as well. For example, I ask participants in each of my semester-length courses to establish, revisit, and maintain group norms for our work together. This process helps students increase their awareness of how they learn, how others learn, and how to engage in creative controversy within the context of civil dialogue. Student affairs educators often teach structured classes (for example, leadership, interpersonal skills, diversity) and more fluid workshops (for example, diversity, alcohol abuse, eating disorders, relationships, and self-esteem) in which this norms process could help students maximize their learning opportunities. Implementing active learning in these contexts is essential if we are truly to engage students in authoring their own perspectives on their identity, relationships, diversity issues, and healthy living habits.

The Resident Assistant Institute demonstrates that how an experience is processed is the key to active learning. Although the institute involved trips off campus, the model is equally viable without an off-campus component. As long as a meaningful experience can be created and the processing follows the tenets of active learning, almost any educational program or workshop can implement active learning. Films, lectures, and performances are a mainstay on most college campuses. Think about the last such event you attended. Most likely it was followed by a short question-and-answer period during which many people departed, a short gathering of a small group of participants who approached the speaker after the formal conclusion, and a few sporadic conversations in the spaces outside the lecture hall. Informal conversations of this sort are valuable; however, they generally involve people with similar perspectives and offer no support for working through conflicting views. Follow-up dialogues in which students could pose problems based on their view of the issue, reflect on the experience, process multiple perspectives about it, organize new understandings, and explore how those apply to their lives could turn these routine campus events into active learning opportunities. Pursuit of these topics from students' vantage points is a crucial part of this process.

Implementing active learning is particularly important in contexts in which students are uncomfortable. Whereas an active learning dialogue on alcohol abuse might readily take place within a student community without facilitation, an active learning dialogue on diversity may be more difficult. Miami University uses an interactive video on race relations to help students explore issues of race. The video, created by members of the communication and educational psychology departments (Miami University Department of Communications, 1991), plays out various scenarios in which race is a factor. Students access the video via a computer and can see the multiple perspectives that emerge as students interact with one another in the scenarios. Discussion facilitators are available for groups to process what they have seen. These discussions are opportunities to implement active learning principles to help students struggle with the difficult issue of race, using students' own views as a starting point. Similarly, service learning settings often involve intense issues such as poverty and social justice. Processing these experiences actively is essential if they are to be meaningfully incorporated into students' lives.

Implications for Good Practice in Student Affairs

Advocating active learning is far more than emphasizing hands-on experience. It is more than changing the follow-up to campus lectures or applying a processing formula to conversations. Using active learning invites students into the center of learning and educational practice. Providing space for them to explore, make decisions, and act on those decisions means making space for mistakes and ambiguity. Just as classroom instructors balk at active learning because students might not "learn the right things," student affairs educators balk at active learning because students might not "learn and do the right things." This call for active learning is a call to revolutionize our thinking about learning, education, and practice.

Indeed, making active learning a principle of good practice in student affairs necessitates asking questions about mission and purposes. Is our mission student learning, as our philosophical roots (for example, Student Personnel Point of View [National Association of Student Personnel Administrators, 1987]) and contemporary leaders (for example, The Student Learning Imperative [American College Personnel Association, 1994]) suggest? Or is our mission service, which has been the historical definition of our place in higher education? Or can service and student learning be merged in a new mission? Student affairs could benefit from an exploration of the degree to which service goals such as providing admission, orientation, housing, financial aid, registration, and the like can be achieved simultaneously with learning goals such as teaching students to weigh options, make informed judgments, and take responsibility for the consequences. It is possible that many services we have traditionally provided also have a learning component. Even financial aid, perceived as primarily a service function, can be structured to teach students financial management. Constructing such a function as a learning context, however, warrants new ways of thinking about staffing and daily operations.

Using active learning also changes criteria for success. The number of students who attended a workshop recedes in value compared to the nature of the experience that occurred for those present. Whether we conducted ten diversity programs this year pales in comparison to whether students who attended were effectively engaged in sharing, reflecting on, and remaking their perspectives on diversity. Honest campus conversation about racial tensions and eating disorders is valued as a marker of success over keeping these campus dynamics secret. Valuing glitches in student group functioning and the learning they produce is more important than maintaining smooth, efficient organizations in which student learning is minimized.

The teaching/learning structures associated with active learning in student affairs have implications far beyond the formats and phases of dialogue that appear on the surface of models such as Community Standards and the RA Institute. Students are partners in these educational processes rather than subjects to which this education is "done." Students are trusted to contribute to the educational goals, which are clearly stated at the outset. Working as teachers-learners (Freire, 1970/1986), student affairs educators let go of control and embrace ambiguity in order to make space at the center of the learning enterprise for students.

I suppose the judicious reader, who has persevered to this point in the chapter, is wondering how on earth student affairs professionals might find time to implement active learning as it is defined here. There are enough daily dilemmas and ambiguities that need resolution as it is; does creating more to promote student learning really make sense? Or in light of the pressure to demonstrate that student affairs contributes to students' education, is it wise to build bridges we know take two or three years to cross? In thinking about these questions, consider the present state of affairs. Most agree that the total undergraduate experience is not what it should be, most lament that students should be more ready than they are for adult responsibility upon leaving college, and the academic side of the house is attempting to move to a learning rather than teaching model, essentially a shift toward the active learning principle that is the topic of this chapter. As far as the most serious campus issues are concerned—violence in relationships, eating disorders, substance abuse, appreciation of diversity—we have little evidence that our concerted efforts are making a major difference. We have substantial evidence, primarily from behavior data and understanding student development, that many students are not developmentally "capable" of appreciating diversity, making healthy decisions about themselves, and managing their conflicts with others. Unless we arrange our practice around their end of the bridge, we will not be able to demonstrate that we make a difference primarily because we may not.

The UNLV Community Standards Model demonstrates that using active learning does not necessarily take more time; it takes spending the time differently. Resident advisers there spend their time facilitating meetings and helping students talk to each other, work through conflicts, and make decisions. This takes the place of time spent by the majority of resident advisers on college campuses on confronting individuals about their behavior and talking with them to try to change it. Similarly, the staff who facilitate the RA Institute spend their time helping students plan and reflect on an experience rather than spending more time planning what might be useful. Perhaps the additional time needed to attach follow-up discussion to campus lectures can be accommodated by offering fewer lectures. Putting time into quality events is wiser than focusing on quantity. Many of the daily dilemmas that consume student affairs staff time are outcomes of students' lack of ability to make informed judgments. Putting our priority on teaching them to do so has the potential to alter the student culture to influence new young members in more positive ways. And finally, even if active learning does take more time in some instances, if we could demonstrate that we accomplished goals consistent with those of most colleges and universities, would that not be worthwhile?

Conclusion

Active learning necessitates new assumptions about learning, knowledge, students, educators, and student affairs practice. Viewing learning as the continual reconstruction of belief in the integration of personal experience and existing knowledge brings students to center stage as partners in learning. Educators take more responsibility for managing the process and less responsibility for controlling the content. As Ira Shor (1992) pointed out, however, that empowering education is not "permissive, nondirected, unstructured" (p. 247). Educators still expose students to existing knowledge and multiple perspectives, and help them learn how to reflect upon and make judgments about existing knowledge. The shift here is that educators focus on teaching students how to make informed judgments they can apply in their lives rather than teaching them what judgments to make. There is a trust inherent in this shift—a trust that students who genuinely explore and reflect on multiple perspectives will construct perspectives that are healthy for themselves and the human community.

3

Helping Students Develop Coherent Values and Ethical Standards

Jon C. Dalton

Good student affairs practice provides opportunities for students, faculty, staff, and student affairs educators to demonstrate the values that define a learning community. Effective learning communities are committed to justice, honesty, equality, civility, freedom, dignity, and responsible citizenship. Such communities challenge students to develop meaningful values for a life of learning. Standards espoused by student affairs divisions should reflect the values that bind the campus community to its educational mission [ACPA and NASPA, 1997, p. 4].

American colleges and universities have traditionally emphasized the importance of teaching students to acquire and utilize knowledge in the context of core values and ethical standards such as justice, equality, civility, freedom, dignity, and responsible citizenship. The conviction that learning has a moral context and that an educated person possesses certain traits of character, including a moral obligation to the common good, is deeply embedded in American higher education.

Recent national reports on education and society have been highly critical of the neglect of values in undergraduate education and have called for renewed attention to the central role of character and civic education in colleges and universities. *Returning to Our Roots: The Student Experience* (National Association of State Universities and Land-Grant Colleges, 1997, p. vi) urges that "Values deserve special attention in this effort. We dare not ignore this obligation in a society that sometimes gives the impression that character and virtues such as tolerance, civility, and personal and social responsibility are discretionary."

In a similar vein, the Report of the Wingspread Group, *An American Imperative: Higher Expectations for Higher Education* (1993a, p. 5) argues for "matters of the spirit" in student learning and development: "But we do argue that faith and deep moral conviction matter in human affairs. Because they do, they must matter on campus."

Much of the recent concern about the character and civility of college students is a reaction to the significant increase in self-interested values and privatism in America's youth over the past twenty-five years (Astin, Green, and Korn, 1987). The ascendancy of self-oriented materialistic values among high school and college students raises troubling questions about their ethical commitment to the common good and their moral inclination to provide future leadership in solving society's most complex human problems. At century's end a national consensus is forming that colleges and universities must play a greater role in helping to solve major societal problems by reaffirming their historic mission of character development and citizenship training.

Concern for students' values and ethical standards is as essential to student affairs practice as responding to fire alarms in the residence halls or confronting underage drinking at fraternity parties. It comes with the territory. Consequently the issue is not whether we should address values and ethical standards in our work with college students but *how* we do it and *for what purposes* we do it.

In this chapter I argue for an approach to good practice in helping students develop coherent values and ethical standards derived from the practical tasks of working with students in contemporary higher education settings. This approach is often referred to as *character development*. In this chapter, I define the concept of character and describe the role student affairs practice plays in its development in students. Next, I identify factors that promote character development and present some practical strategies for promoting it.

The Concept of Character

Part of the debate about how to help students develop coherent values and ethical standards concerns the terms used. The literature on college student development includes terms such as *integrity, moral, citizenship, ethical,* and *values education* to refer to educational efforts to promote student values and ethical standards. In this chapter I use the terms *character* and *character education* to refer to the outcomes and process of promoting coherent values and ethical standards in college. *Character* refers to the habits of mind, heart, and conduct that help students know and do what is ethical. Good character consists of understanding, caring about, and acting upon core ethical values (Lickona, 1976). To be a person of character is to be an individual who chooses to act consistently on the basis of ethical principles.

The concept of character is an old educational term with new relevance for higher education. It is a particularly useful term, since it integrates the dimensions of thinking, feeling, and behavior and stresses the cognitive, emotional, and behavioral dimensions of student development. Character development is consistent with the goal of holistic student development, a guiding principle of student affairs since 1937.

The concept of character is multifaceted. Rest (1975) explains that there are multifaceted interconnections among cognition, affect, and behavior and that efforts to educate morally must take account of the complexity of morality. An analogy might be the concept of health. *Good health* indicates a positive state that is achieved by a complex set of practices and conditions that contribute to a desired state of being. Many argue that good health is primarily a matter of proper diet. Some claim exercise is the key to good health. Still others emphasize the health-producing benefits of positive thinking and meditation.

The concept of character generates a similar debate. Anne Matthews (1997, p. 24) asks, "Is it the point of college to build brains or character? To expose undergraduates to ideas or to the right ideas?" Moral development research suggests that no single educational activity can produce character any more than one single activity can produce good health. The best evidence seems to suggest that character development is the product of a number of critical influences that combine during late adolescence to form a coherent state of belief and behavior we call *character*. Character development is an integral part of an interconnected network of developmental trends that occur in college students (Pascarella and Terenzini, 1991).

Character development is not simply a matter of a single educational activity or program by a college or university. There are no quick "fixes" in the process of fostering coherent values and ethical standards. Rather, character is the result of many educational experiences designed to help students learn moral sentiments, use moral reasoning, moderate self-interest, and behave in a manner consistent with core values and ethical standards.

Higher education cannot bear full responsibility for promoting these outcomes in students but it can make a critical difference in students' education and personal development when they are open to moral influence and learning.

Character Development and Student Affairs Practice

At least four aspects of student affairs practice directly involve character education and development. Student affairs professionals confront these issues in all higher education settings because they are unavoidable in working with college students and are essential for the development of students.

Respect for Truth: Orienting Students to Academic Integrity Standards and Conduct

Although there is often disagreement in the academy about what type of moral education to promote, there is little disagreement that academic integrity and its associated values and behaviors are central to the academic mission of all colleges and universities. Academic integrity is arguably the most important ethical principle in higher education. College students must learn and practice this ethical standard to be successful in higher education. Teaching college students to understand and practice this ethical standard, however, involves more than simply creating rules and punishing violators. It involves instilling a respect for truth and a scrupulous honesty in communicating one's ideas and information. Academic integrity is the bedrock moral standard of the intellectual enterprise of colleges and universities.

Students who cheat do not learn effectively and their behavior undermines the fundamental integrity of the entire academic community. No college or university can tolerate widespread cheating and dishonesty among its students or faculty. Consequently, every college and university must make some effort to inculcate academic integrity standards and conduct to students through educational activities, rules, and policies designed to teach and enforce these core values. The core values include personal honesty, respect for the truth, and the moral courage to resist cheating.

The Ethical Responsibilities of Community: Teaching Students to Live with Others

A second area of character development involves interpersonal relationships among students, faculty, and staff. One of the most important adjustments in college is the experience of living on one's own and learning to appreciate and relate to others who are different. Learning how to live in harmony and practice civility with others whose values, beliefs, and lifestyles differ from one's own presents an important ethical challenge. Students must learn how to balance their personal beliefs and values with respect for the differing beliefs and values of others. Living in a diverse community requires the development and practice of respect for others and their values, civility, responsibility for one's own conduct, equal consideration and treatment of others, tolerance, and the ability to mediate conflicts.

Commitment to the Common Good: Preparing Students for Lives of Civic Responsibility

A third practical area for character development in college is preparing students to be responsible members of society. To accomplish this, students must learn to put into practice the knowledge and values they gain from higher education. College life can insulate students from the outside world and the moral issues of everyday life. Our responsibility is to teach values and behaviors that prepare students for responsible membership in a democratic society. Community service has been embraced by many colleges and universities as a means to help bridge the gap between academic study and social responsibility. Many institutions have developed service-learning programs, community partnership programs, and other forms of community service that enable students to learn about community problems and prepare for active civic participation and responsibility after college.

Civic education and service efforts by colleges and universities focus on the development of moral traits such as respect for others, fairness, commitment to the common good, and social justice—civic virtues that have traditionally been important moral outcomes of higher education.

Ethical Decision Making: Advising and Mentoring Students in Times of Personal Moral Conflict and Crisis

Because student affairs professionals have so much direct interaction with college students they are uniquely situated to help when students struggle with personal moral conflicts. Questions about values and behaviors arise naturally in the context of students' learning and development, and they look to peers and mentors for advice and guidance. Student affairs professionals have many opportunities to help students analyze, clarify, and integrate moral perspectives into their beliefs and behaviors. Whether they choose to respond or not, student affairs professionals will find that they are invited by students to help sort through personal ethical problems and decisions.

In summary, there are four inescapable areas of student affairs practice that involve helping students develop coherent moral values and ethical standards. Students must

1. Learn and practice academic integrity
2. Live responsibly in the community
3. Develop citizenship skills and commitment for life after college
4. Grow and learn from personal moral crises and ethical conflicts

Factors That Promote Character Development in College

Over the past several decades considerable research has been conducted on the learning processes by which individuals develop ethical judgment and behavior. We know much more about the primary factors that promote moral development, although there is disagreement about how these factors interrelate. The following seven factors are known to influence moral development and appear to be critical to understanding how and why character development occurs in college.

Caring for Others

One of the fundamental conditions for ethical development is the ability to consider issues from another's perspective. Unless students are able to empathize with others and gain an appreciation of their thoughts, feelings, and ways of viewing the world, they will be isolated in their own subjectivity. Being involved in situations in which students have responsibility for caring for others can help them to develop insight and sensitivity to the feelings and perspectives of others. Lickona (1976) argues that recognition of others' rights and needs leads naturally to concern about issues of fairness and responsibility. Gilligan's (1982) research on the perspectives unique in women's moral development reveals a special concern for caring for others and taking responsibility for their welfare. Being able to empathize with the perspective of others appears to be a necessary precondition for moral development (Selman, 1976).

Role Modeling

One of the most powerful influences on ethical development is moral example. Heath (1968) found in his research at Haverford College that students' integration of values was strongly influenced by their interaction with staff who served as moral examples. Perry (1970) reached much the same conclusion in his research with students at Harvard. He found that value commitments in college students were directly influenced by educators who themselves had an open style in which their values, doubts, and personal commitments were visible to students.

The power of the moral example is that it conveys values directly through personal commitment and action. Student affairs professionals often serve as role models. They explain procedures, serve as advocates, and provide advice and assistance to students. Students know student affairs professionals and have closer ties to them on campus than anyone other than peers.

Experiences That Challenge One's Ways of Thinking

The encounter and struggle with experiences that challenge one's own beliefs and values can be very influential in promoting character development in college students. Experiences that challenge established ways of thinking and acting often force a reexamination of values. The values that are judged to be inadequate or inconsistent tend to be discarded and new value commitments are confirmed.

Experiences that challenge unexamined beliefs and values are so important to student development that some educators believe that they should be intentionally promoted. Heath (1968) argued that "disorganizing" experiences are very important in challenging the values of students to promote more mature and consistent values. For traditional-age students, the freshman year is an important time because students are especially receptive to the exploration of their inner life and the values and beliefs of others.

In summarizing the analysis of how development occurs in students, Chickering and Reisser (1993) conclude that development occurs through sequences of differentiation and integration. Differentiation requires a challenge or disruption of one's way of thinking. Students' moral thinking must be sufficiently challenged if they are to integrate conflicting values and develop more complex levels of moral reasoning and behavior.

Decision Making

Decision making, in real and hypothetical situations, stimulates moral awareness and development. Mattox (1975) found that discussions and decision making about moral issues are needed for moral growth. Deciding between conflicting alternatives forces students to evaluate their own positions and beliefs. Morrill (1980) believes that an awareness of personal values can be heightened by the process of comparison and contrast, which is stimulated through situations requiring decision making.

There is general agreement in research on moral development that the disequilibrium produced through decisions involving moral conflicts helps to promote moral development. Such situations force individuals to reexamine values and beliefs and test their adequacy in the face of challenging moral situations.

College Peer Culture

Any serious effort to promote the moral and civic character of students during college must, at some point, come to terms with the powerful, shaping influence of college peer culture. Like an invisible invader, the influences of the peer culture permeate almost all aspects of students' lives and erode or enhance the best educational efforts of faculty and administrators. Astin's (1993) research on college students found that the single most important source of influence on the individual student is the peer group. Despite the sophisticated efforts of colleges and universities to guide and shape students' values and moral development during college, most of these characteristics move in the direction of the dominant peer group orientation.

College peer culture is shaped by influences external to the campus, especially at larger institutions. Horowitz (1987) observed that much of student culture has become isolated from the intellectual life of institutions. The typical image of college held by today's undergraduate is substantially influenced by the youth culture as portrayed by the mass media.

The shift of college peer culture away from the campus has made it much more difficult for colleges and universities to transmit values and foster character development. To have any significant influence on the moral development of college students, student affairs staff must understand and take advantage of the positive power of peer groups while also minimizing the negative undertow of the popular media.

Experience of Community

Students' experience with a supportive sense of community in an educational setting can contribute substantially to the development of their values. A community support system makes it easier for students to experiment and take risks.

Levine (1980) points out that one important measure of community is how strongly students believe they can profit from cooperation from the community. If students do not identify with the values of the community, they will not be inclined to regard them as significant in their own lives.

Students' perceptions of community are also influenced by how they are treated in the community. Hersh, Mills, and Fielding (1980) surveyed 800 students about critical events that occurred to them in the educational community. Students identified consideration of other's needs, feelings, and interests as important positive factors.

Encountering Diversity

An important factor in promoting ethical awareness and development in students is the experience of being confronted and challenged by others' values and lifestyles. Such experiences tend to encourage and even demand reflectiveness and reexamination of what one may know or believe. Students who are isolated or resist encounters with others who hold contrasting values are likely to be rigidly tied to an unexamined set of values. Values that are unexamined may be superficial and self-serving.

In their study of students in the Sierra Project, Resnikoff and Jennings (1982) found that experiences with others that presented a discrepancy of values and beliefs tended to promote changes in moral reasoning. Learning how to disagree with another's values and beliefs without rejecting them was an important means of clarifying and testing one's own values. Interacting with others whose values are different helps one to move beyond self-interest and egocentrism to higher levels of moral reflection and social role taking.

Practical Strategies for Promoting Character Development in Students

Many different educational strategies have been used in higher education to promote the ethical development of students. These strategies address the seven factors of moral development in different ways, depending upon the institutional mission and setting. The educational strategies range from highly structured, religion-based programs in private institutions with a faith-centered mission to large, public research universities with student conduct regulations designed to inhibit academic cheating and social conflict but in most other respects leaving students on their own. Since character development is a complex developmental process that encompasses a number of essential learning and maturational factors, there is probably no one single educational approach that works best in all situations. Rather, there are several. I propose five basic educational strategies that are widely used to promote ethical development during the college years: transmission, clarification, moral reasoning, moral commitment, and moral action.

These strategies provide a comprehensive educational framework for student affairs that is suitable for use in all types of colleges and universities and that addresses all of the critical moral factors in ethical development discussed above. Although any one of the strategies can make a positive contribution to students' ethical development, all five strategies should be included in any comprehensive institutional effort to promote ethical development.

Values Transmission

The purpose of the values transmission strategy is to instill or inculcate in students the institutional core values that are considered essential for campus life (Figure 3.1). Every college and university embraces some essential values that they believe every student must learn and practice, though these essential values may vary from institution to institution. These core values are most often conveyed in student conduct rules, college regulations, and institutional policies and practices. Institutions transmit values most directly through their formal regulations and guidelines that define ethical conduct and acceptable behavior. Institutions also publicly transmit values through symbols, rituals, traditions, and role modeling. Through all of these means, colleges and universities seek to pass on to students certain fundamental values believed to be essential for ethical life and conduct during college and beyond.

Among the great variety of values that institutions convey to students are some values that almost all colleges and universities seek to transmit: academic honesty, respect for others, personal re-

Figure 3.1. Transmitting Values.

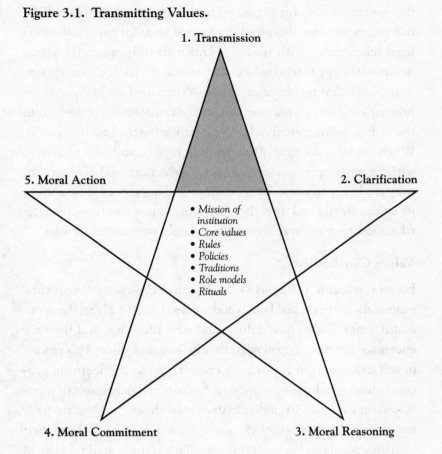

1. Transmission

5. Moral Action

2. Clarification

- Mission of
  institution
- Core values
- Rules
- Policies
- Traditions
- Role models
- Rituals

4. Moral Commitment

3. Moral Reasoning

sponsibility, social cooperation, fairness, and commitment to the common good. As argued earlier, these values are essential for campus life and democratic citizenship, and to a greater or lesser extent all colleges and universities are engaged in transmitting them.

The clear and effective transmission of values is important for college students, since this is the chief means by which students learn what is important to believe and how one should behave in the institution. Typically colleges and universities go to great lengths to communicate their values and standards to students through a variety of formal documents and pronouncements. These documents are not only important in defining standards for students' moral conduct but also provide a formal basis for the institution's legal relationship with students. Unfortunately, when the transmission strategy is used as the sole means of character education, some significant problems can result. When used exclusively as the primary means of promoting values, the transmission strategy runs the risk of being perceived as indoctrinating and authoritarian. When students are simply told what to believe and how to behave without active personal engagement, reflection, and exploration, they are likely to resist. Every college and university must convey its values clearly and directly to students, but promoting character education requires much more than simply transmitting values.

Values Clarification

For most students, college is a time of considerable self-reflection and examination of personal beliefs and values (Figure 3.2). Students encounter new ideas, new values, and new lifestyles, and they are encouraged to reflect upon what they believe and value. This process of self-examination is not only encouraged in the learning process of undergraduate education, it is also a practical result of interaction on campus with individuals of great diversity. Most students are eager to learn what others think and believe and to share their own viewpoints and convictions, especially if they can do this in an atmosphere of low risk and personal trust. The values clarification strategy has been used for decades as an educational method for helping students to explore their own values and the values of others in a manner that is nonthreatening and nonjudgmental. It is a very popular strategy with students because it is open and nondirective and can be used in a variety of settings on campus to help students get to know each other and explore personal values.

At its best the clarification strategy provides powerful learning opportunities for students to reflect upon their own values through a process of comparing and contrasting them with the beliefs and values of their peers. The values clarification literature is rich with

Figure 3.2. Clarifying Values.

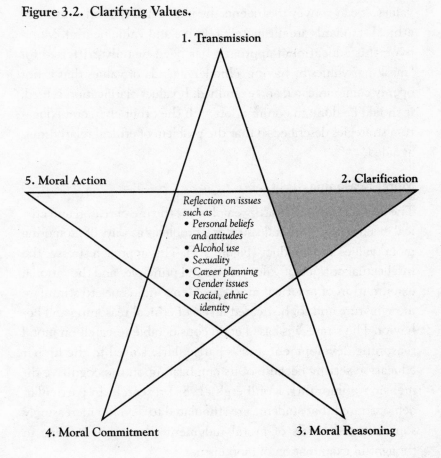

*Reflection on issues
such as*
- *Personal beliefs
  and attitudes*
- *Alcohol use*
- *Sexuality*
- *Career planning*
- *Gender issues*
- *Racial, ethnic
  identity*

1. Transmission

2. Clarification

3. Moral Reasoning

4. Moral Commitment

5. Moral Action

a variety of practical activities and material that can be used in many ways on campus, such as new student orientation, leadership training, residence halls programming, and student activities. This educational approach is popular with student affairs professionals because it avoids the appearance of being indoctrinating or "preachy" to students about values.

A significant problem with exclusive or primary use of this strategy is that it is value-free or morally neutral. Since values clarification avoids transmitting specific values and is nonjudgmental about values, it can convey to students the impression that all values and ethical standards are ultimately relative and value neutral. Moreover, this educational approach has been heavily criticized for "masking" values by having a hidden agenda of values that is not openly communicated and examined. If values clarification is used, it should be done in conjunction with the other character education strategies described so that the problem of ethical relativism is avoided.

Moral Reasoning

The moral reasoning strategy emphasizes the use of reason and critical examination of moral issues and problems as ways of promoting moral values and conduct (Figure 3.3). This approach stresses the intellectual critique of values and moral principles and the rational examination of practical moral problems and issues to stimulate more mature and sophisticated levels of ethical reasoning and behavior. The strategy is based upon considerable research on moral reasoning development and is particularly suited to the higher education setting because of its emphasis upon the cognitive dimension of morality. Kohlberg's (1984) research, in particular, demonstrated that students are stimulated to develop increasingly sophisticated levels of moral judgment when they engage in thoughtful examination of moral issues.

Student affairs staff who use this strategy often draw on real-life ethical problems from the experiences of students to construct moral dilemmas for discussion and critique by students. This is a particularly effective technique in training students for roles such as serving on the judicial board, honor code board, as peer counselors, residence halls advisers, and in leadership training. Engaging students in thoughtful examination of engaging moral problems over an extended period can be a powerful educational strategy for enhancing moral reasoning.

One of the limitations of moral reasoning is its rather narrow focus on the cognitive aspects of morality. This strategy uses rea-

Figure 3.3. Moral Reasoning.

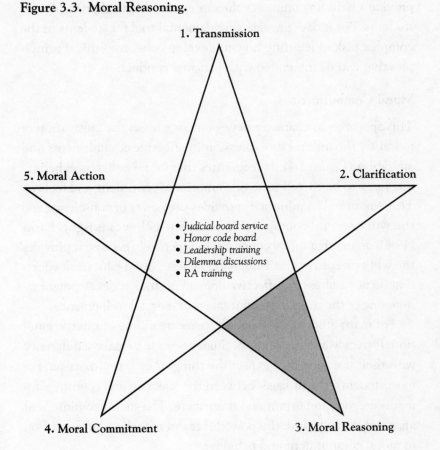

1. Transmission

5. Moral Action

2. Clarification

- *Judicial board service*
- *Honor code board*
- *Leadership training*
- *Dilemma discussions*
- *RA training*

4. Moral Commitment

3. Moral Reasoning

soning skills and rational examination of moral situations as the primary means for promoting ethical awareness and maturity. Student affairs educators should note that moral reasoning does not address some important domains of morality such as moral imagination, moral sentiment, inculcation of values and ethical standards, moral conscience, and moral conduct. This educational approach also has been criticized for gender bias in its research base. Moreover, helping students to reason at more mature levels of ethical thinking does not necessarily result in greater personal commitment to do what is right or to live a more ethical life. Neither does moral reasoning provide a basis for common values or essential ethical principles for students. But it does provide a fundamental tool for students in the complex task of learning how to develop coherent ethical principles that can be integrated with personal conduct.

Moral Commitment

This approach to character development stresses the cultivation of moral sentiment and its expression in affective commitments and affiliation (Figure 3.4). It recognizes that moral beliefs and behaviors need to be rooted in strong emotional sentiment and feeling. This emotional commitment provides the power of conscience and the will or moral courage to do what one believes is right. Parks (1990) argues that moral courage is indispensable because it provides the will power to act on values and beliefs. Moral education efforts that do not address the affective domain of student development ignore one of the most important facets of moral development.

For many students, the college years are a time of intense emotional struggle and maturation. Students want to make a difference with their lives and they expect the things they learn to matter. For most students, the linkages between the affective and cognitive domains are very important and immediate. The moral commitment approach seeks to link the powerful realm of feelings and emotion to moral commitment and behavior.

Faith-oriented colleges and universities emphasize this strategy through religious activities such as worship, prayer, confession, and fasting. Many secular colleges and universities emphasize moral commitment through literature and the arts, social justice activities, and community service. This educational strategy is sometimes controversial in secular institutions because of its strong emphasis upon pressing students to explore and make personal commitments to beliefs and values. But it does not have to be indoctrinating simply because of the effort to help students to root their beliefs and values in personal conscience and conviction. If moral education does not address this powerful realm of student development, it will have little lasting influence.

Figure 3.4. Moral Commitment.

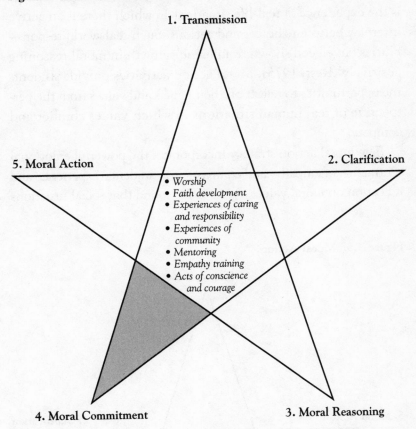

1. Transmission

5. Moral Action

2. Clarification

- Worship
- Faith development
- Experiences of caring
  and responsibility
- Experiences of
  community
- Mentoring
- Empathy training
- Acts of conscience
  and courage

4. Moral Commitment

3. Moral Reasoning

Moral Action

The moral action strategy emphasizes student involvement in real-life situations that require responsibility and action (Figure 3.5). Student affairs staff who use this approach seek to expose students to circumstances in which they can experience real-life problems and take responsibility for helping and caring for others.

The moral action strategy does not attempt to inculcate values directly or to establish some values as preferable to others. Rather, this approach is based on the premise that values are internalized only as an individual moves beyond thinking and feeling to action.

Consequently, the critical factor in this moral education strategy is the experience of real-life situations in which there is an active interplay between choices and actions. Such real-world responsibilities have been shown to influence growth in moral reasoning positively (Rest, 1975). Moral action activities provide students the opportunities to reflect on their beliefs and values from the perspective of real human situations in which values conflict and compete.

The moral action strategy incorporates the powerful emotional sentiments of empathy and compassion in students' experience and reflection on moral values. Rest (1979) found that social situations

Figure 3.5. Moral Action.

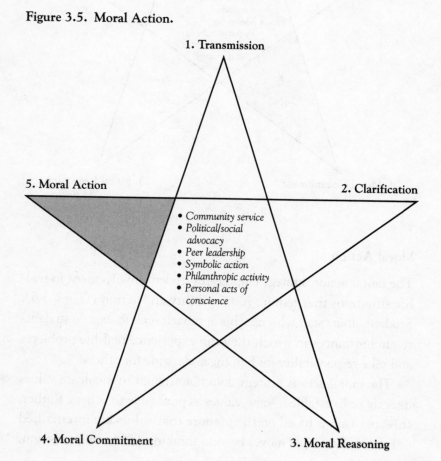

1. Transmission

5. Moral Action

2. Clarification

- Community service
- Political/social advocacy
- Peer leadership
- Symbolic action
- Philanthropic activity
- Personal acts of conscience

4. Moral Commitment

3. Moral Reasoning

can arouse strong feelings even before one understands a situation rationally. The moral action approach seeks intentionally to involve students in real-life situations in which empathy will be aroused.

Reflections on Chickering's Seventh Vector of Identity

Chickering and Reisser (1993) identified integrity as the seventh and final vector of college student development. Perhaps they chose it as the final vector because ethical integrity represents the culminating achievement of student development in college. In the nineteenth century it was common for college presidents to teach a senior capstone course on moral philosophy because they believed that integrating knowledge within a framework of ethical values should be the culminating educational experience in college.

There is no single educational formula for helping students develop the seventh vector. In many respects, the development of character is one of the most challenging and complex tasks of higher education. But character development is by no means an esoteric or impossible educational enterprise. It is fostered through an educational environment that clearly transmits core values and behavioral standards, provides visible role models, helps students reflect on and clarify values, gives students practical opportunities to act on their convictions and beliefs, and provides a caring, supportive community. An educational environment for character development should include the following activities and educational arrangements:

1. A mission statement that articulates core values and virtues

2. A general education curriculum that includes core values and virtues as educational outcomes

3. An academic honor code

4. A student conduct code that defines student rights, duties, and responsible citizenship

5. A student compact, creed, or statement that articulates the institution's core values and virtues and that students are expected to affirm as part of their membership in the campus community

6. Formal incentives and structured opportunities for community service and community-building activities

7. A campus ethos of welcoming and caring for students

8. New student programs that orient and introduce new students to campus resources, traditions, core values, role models, and help establish friendships and affiliation with the institution

9. Campus governance structures that provide for active student participation and responsibility

10. Consistent role modeling by university leaders to affirm the core values and virtues of the institution

11. A visible and effective program of rewards and recognition for exemplary students who model core values and virtues

12. Recognition and support for students' spiritual and religious expression and development

13. Structured opportunities on campus for public discussion and debate about values and moral issues.

Dewey (1950) wrote that the highest achievement in education is a free and powerful character. Dewey's conviction that education must help shape human character is a compelling reminder about the challenging work of student affairs in higher education to help students develop coherent values and ethical standards. For many student affairs staff, the work of character education is one of the most challenging and rewarding aspects of their work with college students. It has been for me.

4

Setting the Bar High to Promote Student Learning

George D. Kuh

Student learning is enhanced when expectations for student performance inside and outside the classroom are high, appropriate to students' abilities and aspirations, and consistent with the institution's
mission and philosophy. Expectations should address the wide range
of student behaviors associated with academic achievement, intellectual and psychosocial development, and individual and community responsibility. Good student affairs divisions systematically
describe desired levels of performance to students as well as to practitioners and regularly assess whether their performances are consistent with institutional expectations [ACPA and NASPA, 1997, p. 4].

"Expect more and you will get more" (Chickering and Gamson,
1987b, p. 5). This aphorism reflects the widespread belief that to
achieve excellence at all levels of education—preschool through
postsecondary—we need to challenge all students to meet high performance standards. Setting the bar high motivates people to achieve
their potential and surpass their self-perceived limits. Expecting a
lot from students has positive effects not only for the bright and
highly motivated, but also for "the poorly prepared [and] those un-
willing to exert themselves" (Chickering and Gamson, 1987b, p. 5).

An expectation represents a look ahead in anticipation of some
future event or condition. For example, many traditional-age, first-
year college students have an idea that college life will be different

in some ways than high school: They relish the prospect of being on their own, free from the supervision of parents and family; they think they will work harder and study more than they did in high school; they look forward to making new friends. Many older students who have been in the workforce for some years expect that their courses will present information that will improve their job performance and advancement prospects.

Faculty and student affairs staff have expectations, too. Some of these expectations relate to their own performance and relations with one another, and others pertain to students. With respect to the latter, faculty members expect students to attend class, complete assignments on time, and take responsibility for their own learning. Student affairs professionals expect students to abide by the institution's rules and regulations and participate in out-of-class activities that enrich the undergraduate experience and contribute to the welfare of the campus and surrounding community. To determine whether their performance is acceptable, institutions use academic standards and community conduct codes to evaluate and give feedback to students.

Expectations shape the formation and attainment of aspirations and goals. Aspirations represent a strong desire to achieve at a high level, such as graduating with academic honors, playing intercollegiate sports, or singing in a touring concert choir. Goals represent specific ends toward which effort is directed. Some goals may be learning-related, such as mastering a body of knowledge, acquiring expertise in software development, or reading and speaking a foreign language. Other goals may be utilitarian, such as earning a lot of money after graduation. Students who aspire to become a physician or an attorney will be disappointed if they underestimate the amount of time they need to study and subsequently fail to meet the academic standards established by their college or the admission criteria of medical or law schools.

People, especially newcomers, have difficulty expressing expectations with a high degree of specificity. High school seniors are able to describe in general terms what college will be like but have trouble articulating specifically what they will do on a daily basis or what will happen to them; first-generation students in particular lack the tacit knowledge about college life that other students acquire from family members (Hossler, Schmit, Vesper, forthcoming). At the same time, expectations play a critical role in making sense of new situations as they help students (as well as faculty and student affairs staff) deal with the ambiguity inherent in new environments. As Weick (1995, p. 148) explained:

> People do not have much to start with when their goal is to "get to know" some other person, or setting, or job. This means that their expectations cannot help but be a force that shapes the world they try to size up. They see things of their own making. They see what they expect. . . . When a person compares an event with an expectation . . . noticing becomes focused. The expectation affects the information that is selected for processing (for example, Snyder and Swann, 1978), the inferences that are made (Cantor and Mischel, 1977), and the information that is retained (for example, Zadny and Gerard, 1974).

This view suggests that if institutions can specify in advance their expectations for desired behaviors, such as high academic achievement and harmonious social relations, students will be more likely to perform accordingly because they are better prepared to attend to, interpret, and remember actions and events when they get to college (Weick, 1995).

In this chapter I examine the role of expectations in enhancing the quality of undergraduate education, with specific implications for student affairs. After clarifying key terms and reviewing some of the pertinent literature and research, I discuss how student affairs in partnership with faculty members, academic administrators, and students can enhance student learning by establishing high expectations for students' performances, inside and outside the classroom.

Research on Expectations and Learning

Expectations and performance are positively linked. Though most of the research about expectations in educational settings focuses on classroom behavior and academic achievement in elementary and secondary schools, these studies show moderate to high correlations (.5 to .9) between instructor expectations and student achievement (Jussim, 1986). For example, in Catholic schools characterized by uniformly high achievement expectations for all students, disadvantaged and minority students have frequently performed exceedingly well compared with their counterparts enrolled at other types of schools. High academic expectations are not the only reason for the success of parochial schools, as they also spend more of their resources on instruction compared with public schools (Ravitch, 1996).

Another explanation for the positive relationship between expectations and achievement is the Pygmalion effect or self-fulfilling prophecy, whereby an instructor evokes levels of student performance consistent with the instructor's expectations (Rosenthal and Jacobson, 1968). Teachers who believe their students can achieve at high levels have higher expectations for themselves as well as the students, and make extra efforts to help students succeed, often with remarkable results. Rosenthal (1993) expressed this as affect/effort theory:

> A change in the level of expectation held by a teacher for the intellectual performance of a student is translated into (1) a change in the affect shown by the teacher toward that student and, relatively independently, (2) a change in the degree of effort exerted by the teacher in teaching that student. Specifically, the more favorable

the change in the level of expectation held by the
teacher for a particular student, the more positive the affect shown toward that student and the greater the effort
expended on behalf of that student. [p. 1]

Affect/effort theory is consistent with *The Student Personnel Point
of View* (American Council on Education [ACE], 1949) and research from a variety of disciplines (for example, neurobiology, anthropology, cognitive science, education) (Marchese, 1997) that
shows that attending to the whole person—the affective domain as
well as intellectual functioning—can have a salutary effect on learning and personal development.

The Role of Expectations in Higher Education

The value of high expectations in higher education has been un-
equivocally endorsed in four reports issued within the past fifteen
years. The first, *Involvement in Learning* (Study Group on Conditions of Excellence in Higher Education [Study Group], 1984), was
the higher education community's initial response to *A Nation at
Risk* (National Commission on Excellence in Education, 1983), a
document that called for intense scrutiny of the entire United
States educational system. High expectations was one of three keys
to improving undergraduate education described in *Involvement in
Learning*; the other two ingredients were student involvement in educationally purposeful activities and the combination of regular assessment and prompt feedback. According to the Study Group
(1984), students attempt to meet the expectations that faculty set
for them, provided the expectations are reasonable. To have the intended effect, however, expectations must be public; students and
others "must know not only what is expected [for example, course
and program requirements], but how well it is to be performed"
(Study Group, 1984, p. 20).

The second report, "Principles of Good Practice in Undergraduate Education" (Chickering and Gamson, 1987b), is one of the

most widely disseminated documents in American higher education. Its sixth principle is that "good practice communicates high expectations." For faculty, this means clarifying expectations orally and in writing, designing assignments that challenge and engage students for longer periods on activities that relate to course goals, holding students accountable for the quality of their academic efforts, and encouraging them to go beyond minimum course requirements, such as doing additional reading and writing (Seven Principles Resource Center, 1989).Students have responsibilities, too, such as setting personal learning goals, trying their best in each class, and using institutional resources that pertain to their classes and learning goals (Student Inventory, Principles for Good Practice in Undergraduate Education, 1989). Other compilations of good practices also feature high expectations, addressing diverse activities such as service learning (Mintz and Hesser, 1996), assessment (American Association for Higher Education, 1992), and electronic degree and certificate programs (Western Cooperative for Educational Communications, 1996).

The third report was *An American Imperative: Higher Expectations for Higher Education* (The Wingspread Group on Higher Education [Wingspread Group], 1993a). As with *Involvement in Learning*, the Wingspread report was intended to be a clarion call to improve the quality of undergraduate education. Written by a small group of business, government, and academic leaders, its opening paragraph set a dramatic tone, not unlike the language in *A Nation at Risk*: "A disturbing and dangerous mismatch exists between what American society needs of higher education and what it is receiving. Nowhere is the mismatch more dangerous than in the quality of undergraduate preparation. . . . The American imperative for the twenty-first century is that society must hold higher education to much higher expectations or risk national decline" (Wingspread Group, 1993a, p. 1).

This statement rang true to policymakers and institutional leaders, prompting campus-based dialogues on the three areas of undergraduate education highlighted in the report: taking values seriously, putting student learning first, and creating a nation of learners.

Finally, in *Making Quality Count*, the Education Commission of the States (1995) added five principles to the original seven presented by Chickering and Gamson (1987a, 1987b) for a total of twelve attributes of good practice in undergraduate education. High expectations was listed first: "Students learn more effectively when expectations for learning are placed at high but attainable levels, and when these expectations are communicated clearly from the onset. . . . [W]hen students are expected to take risks and perform at high levels, they make greater effort to succeed" (Education Commission of the States, 1995, p. 17).

Making Quality Count is based on ideas and research discussed in more detail by Ewell and Jones (1996). Their monograph is an excellent resource for infusing good practices in undergraduate education throughout a college or university.

Research on Expectations and Learning in Higher Education

Taken together, these reports and the views of other experts (Banta and Associates, 1993; Blake, Evenbeck, and Melodia, 1997; Chickering and Reisser, 1993; Kuh, Schuh, Whitt, and Associates, 1991; Shattuck, 1997) indicate widespread support for setting high, clearly defined expectations for student and institutional performance. Such enthusiasm is somewhat surprising, however, as very few studies directly address the relationship between expectations and student performance in colleges and universities (Lund, 1995; National Center for Higher Education Management Systems, 1994; Sorcinelli, 1991; Study Group, 1984). Much of the support for higher expectations for higher education assumes that the results of studies of elementary and secondary school student achievement, such as those previously mentioned, are generalizable to higher education settings. Anecdote and personal experience also contribute to near-unanimous support for high expectations. Experienced faculty and student affairs professionals know, or have heard about, students with a history of below-average grades and test scores who excelled in one or more aspects of college life, out-performing others with more impressive backgrounds. The small amount of research that does exist tends to corroborate such observations, especially when the fit between the student and the institutional environment is good (Hossler, Bean, and Associates, 1990).

Student ratings of instruction also provide empirical support for the link between expectations and performance. "Contrary to faculty belief . . . students give higher ratings to difficult courses in which they have to work hard" (Sorcinelli, 1991, p. 21). At Harvard, faculty who set rigorous standards and demanded high quality work were appreciated and highly respected by their students (Light, 1992). Other research shows that students who viewed their instructors as well prepared and organized had greater cognitive gains at the end of the first year of college (Pascarella, Edison, Nora, Hagedorn, and Braxton, 1995); perhaps this is because in well-managed courses students experience less ambiguity in the learning environment and are able to focus their effort on valued tasks and activities that lead to desired outcomes.

In their review of the research on the impact of college on students, Pascarella and Terenzini (1991) did not address the potential link between expectations and intellectual development, knowledge acquisition, or social-emotional development outcomes. But they did acknowledge the educational benefits of the "socialization function" (Pascarella and Terenzini, 1991, p. 650) of activities such as orientation, implying that students who learn about the institution (and, presumably, what is expected of them) prior to beginning classes have a better understanding of what they need to do to succeed in college.

An institution's environment also shapes expectations. Most studies that take into account campus climate and cultural properties do not directly examine the links between expectations and learning. Some research suggests that perceptions of aspects of the institution such as the quality of relationships between students and faculty, or institutional emphasis on critical thinking, shape student expectations, which, in turn, affect student satisfaction and academic performance. For example, results from the National Study of Student Learning (NSSL) show that after controlling for initial differences, students at historically black colleges and universities (HBCUs) realized the same level of learning outcomes and intellectual development at the end of the first year of college as did their white counterparts at other institutions (Bohr, Pascarella, Nora, and Terenzini, 1995). As Fleming (1984) and Allen (1987) pointed out, faculty and staff at HBCUs tend to believe all their students can succeed, tell them they are expected to do so, and provide support and encouragement to inspire them to high levels of performance. The almost-legendary science achievements of graduates of Xavier University of Louisiana (Andreas, 1991) and Oakes College of the University of California at Santa Cruz (J. H. Blake, personal communication, December 2, 1997) are additional evidence of the positive results of expecting students to achieve high levels of academic performance.

What Students Expect from College

A significant challenge to establishing and maintaining high expectations for students is reconciling faculty and staff perceptions and attitudes with students' characteristics and expectations for college and for themselves. For example, only about a third of all faculty involved in undergraduate teaching identify financial wealth as important (Sax, Astin, Arredondo, and Korn, 1996), whereas almost three-quarters of entering first-year students value this goal (Sax, Astin, Korn, and Mahoney, 1995). About twice as many faculty (79 percent) (Sax et al., 1996) as students (42 percent) (Sax et al., 1995) say it is important to develop a meaningful philosophy of life. At one university, 80 percent of incoming students, but only 20 percent of faculty, considered career preparation to be a very important outcome of college (Olsen, 1997).

The gap between student and faculty perceptions of students' academic preparation can be enormous. Less than a quarter of the faculty (24 percent) think students have the academic preparation for college-level work (Sax et al., 1996). Yet more than 40 percent of students expect to earn at least a B average in college (Sax et al., 1995). Students are studying less in high school than did previous cohorts, yet record numbers are graduating from high school with grades of B or better (Sax et al., 1995).

Results over the past decade from the College Student Experiences Questionnaire (CSEQ) national research program show an increase in grades but a decrease in the amount of effort students devote to educationally purposeful activities. Average college grades have risen: about 42 percent of students in the mid-1990s reported B+ or better grades compared with only about 35 percent in the mid-1980s. However, the number of students devoting at least forty hours a week to academics—the total amount of time attending class and studying—dropped an average of 7 percent. At one university, 75 percent of entering students devoted ten or fewer hours per week to their high school studies; only 20 percent planned to study more than twenty hours per week at the university (Olsen, 1997), a figure corroborated by other studies showing that students enrolled full-time study an average of eight to twelve hours a week (and watch television twenty hours per week) (Sax et al., 1995). These data indicate an academic effort shortfall of at least ten hours per week, assuming that students should study about two hours for every hour in class to attain the learning objectives of the average college course.

This trend in diminished effort also extended to the formal extracurriculum, such as involvement in campus organizations and student union activities. In only two areas—writing and use of recreational sports facilities—was student effort higher in the mid-1990s than in the mid-1980s (Kuh, 1997a). Finally, in their study of student experiences with three best practices in undergraduate education (faculty-student interaction, peer cooperation, active learning; Chickering and Gamson, 1987a, 1987b), Kuh and Vesper (1997) found that, at doctoral universities, the amount of student-faculty interaction and active learning decreased between 1990 and 1994.

As a group, these trends and data indicate a gap between what institutions say they want from their students and what students do, or are prepared to do, when they get to college; students, as an aggregate, have much lower expectations of themselves than colleges have of their students. This, of course, adds to the challenge of establishing higher expectations for students and for institutional performance (Education Commission of the States, 1995; Study Group, 1984; Wingspread Group, 1993a).

The Role of Student Affairs in Setting High Expectations

The impact of college is most powerful when policies, practices, and expectations are complementary across in-class and out-of-class learning settings (Pascarella and Terenzini, 1991; Terenzini, Pascarella, and Blimling, 1996). This means that expectations for student performance in formal instructional settings (classrooms, laboratories, studios) and out-of-class venues (residence halls, student government, social organizations, employment settings, playing fields) must be consistently high, clearly articulated, and reinforced by faculty, student affairs professionals, student leaders, and others (Chickering and Gamson, 1987a, 1987b; Education Commission of the States, 1995; Kuh et al., 1991). The student affairs profession has long embraced this goal (American College Personnel Association [ACPA], 1994; American Council on Education, 1949; Brown, 1972; National Association of Student Personnel Administrators [NASPA], 1987).

In this section, a five-step agenda is presented that addresses aspects of institutional functioning that must be considered in order to establish high expectations for students outside the classroom, and to provide feedback about their performance to insure that the expectations are met. The steps are adapted from the ecosystem model of campus redesign (Banning, 1989), and they sketch the territory that must be covered for a division of student affairs to do its part in challenging students to get the most out of their college experience.

At the same time, the steps can be successful only if faculty members, academic administrators, students, and others are involved as well. Impetus for action can begin anywhere in the institution, but effective action requires collaboration. Depending on the institutional context and the nature of cross-institutional relationships, however, some work on building cooperation and encouraging communication might be needed even before the five-step agenda can be implemented. At the very least, strong presidential support is needed to begin and maintain the dialogues that moving through this agenda requires.

Step 1. Determine What the Institution Wants to Expect of Its Students

Through the late 1960s, the doctrine of *in loco parentis* guided student-institution relations at most four-year colleges and universities. Whether parietal rules promoted student learning and personal development is not known, though such institutional regulations made it easier for colleges and universities to specify desired behaviors. However, since the successful legal challenges to *in loco parentis*, most campuses have not had a coherent philosophy with regard to the desired relationship between students and the institution. Hence for many colleges and universities, the first step in raising expectations is to decide the appropriate institutional expectations for today's students and the philosophical and ethical assumptions that undergird the expectations and guide institutional action.

Getting a majority of people on any campus to agree on appropriate expectations for student performance is a complicated task, for at least two reasons. First, the scale and complexity of many in-stitutions makes such an effort appear daunting even to the most optimistic. Through the 1950s, few colleges enrolled more than 15,000 students; about half of all undergraduates attended small col-leges that had denominational ties and distinctive value orienta-tions. Today, three-quarters of all undergraduates attend public universities, many of which are large and complex; the majority of students live off campus. In such settings, it is especially difficult to cultivate a coherent set of values to guide institutional policies, pro-grams, and practices and to articulate consistent messages about ex-pectations. Even more difficult is convincing faculty and staff to change their behavior in ways that encourage and support students to put forth more effort in activities that matter to their education. In fact, channeling student effort toward educationally purposeful activities means not only changing how students spend their time but also how faculty and student affairs professionals spend their time. I shall return to this point later.

Second, once an institution determines what it believes to be appropriately high expectations, it cannot simply set the bar higher and tell students to jump. As explained earlier, expectations, aspi-rations, goals, standards, and student performance are related. Re-search shows that expectations and the performance standards used to provide feedback to students must consider students' character-istics and the institution's mission and educational purposes. For ex-ample, what is considered an appropriate level of participation in campus-based out-of-class activities (for example, clubs and orga-nizations) for full-time, enrolled, traditional-age students does not necessarily apply to older, part-time students who have jobs and families and are involved with community activities.

To help institutions and students discern and clearly articulate appropriately high expectations for student performance, the Na-tional Association of Student Personnel Administrators (NASPA) (Kuh, Lyons, Miller, and Trow, 1995) developed a set of proposi-tions that can be used to engage relevant parties in conversations that could lead to establishing "reasonable expectations." *Reason-ableness* implies a level of student involvement in a variety of in-class and out-of-class venues that is likely to result in high levels of academic achievement and community responsibility. The propo-sitions cover five areas: (1) teaching and learning; (2) the curricu-lum; (3) institutional integrity; (4) the quality of campus life; and (5) educational services.

Drake University (Iowa) used the NASPA document to struc-ture discussions among faculty, students, and administrators about their expectations of one another. North Dakota State University (NDSU) redesigned its admissions and orientation materials and programs to make newcomers aware of the institution's expectations for their conduct. Admissions staff at NDSU talk about what the university expects during presentations to prospective students and their families. Orientation packets contain a summary of NDSU's version of "reasonable expectations," and the president mentions those expectations when welcoming parents and students. Then the vice president for student affairs illustrates the institution's expec-tations with overheads of concrete examples from campus life. In small groups facilitated by upper-division students, students discuss their expectations for college in the context of the institution's expectations.

At Canisius College (New York), *Reasonable Expectations* (Kuh, Lyons, et al., 1994) prompted a series of meetings among the insti-tution's trustees, administrators, faculty, and students. One partic-ularly effective approach was displaying on a matrix comparisons between the college's espoused expectations for students in some key areas of campus life (for example, student participation in cul-tural events, class attendance, alcohol use) and institutional data about actual student behaviors. Students, faculty, and staff discussed with trustees the extent to which institutional information about students was accurate and whether institutional expectations were being met. This exercise allowed the various stakeholders to learn more about one another and to establish a frame of reference for subsequent collaborative efforts to focus institutional effort on things that mattered to undergraduate experiences.

Many other approaches to clarifying expectations can be effective as well. For example, the division of student affairs at Oregon State University used the six principles of campus community described in the Carnegie Foundation for the Advancement of Teaching (1990) report to shape the division's role in influencing student behavior in ways appropriate to an academic environment. At the University of South Carolina the student affairs division took the lead in developing a statement of community standards that subsequently became known as the Carolinian Creed. An excellent example of using institutional values to clarify expectations is Earlham College's (Indiana) Community Code, a compact for campus life that is rooted in the institution's Quaker tradition (Krehbiel and Strange, 1991). Olivet College in Michigan recently developed a compact for campus life consistent with its mission, Education for Individual and Social Responsibility. The Olivet case is particularly interesting because several years ago the college was stunned by a series of racially charged incidents. Olivet has since rebounded due in large part to clarifying its mission, affirming institutional values, and establishing community standards that reflect its mission and values (M. S. Bassis, personal communication, February 6, 1997).

Step 2. Discover What Expectations for Student Performance the Institution Actually Communicates

In all likelihood, recently revised or clarified institutional expectations for student performance will differ in some ways from the expectations that some (or many) faculty and student affairs professionals have for students. For this reason, the expectations actually communicated to students must be determined. This effort can be included in the data collection phase of an institution-wide assessment and improvement initiative or designed as an independent activity. In either case, the project is most likely to produce useful data and have the desired effects if student affairs staff collaborate with colleagues from the institutional research office, campus curriculum committee, and campus assessment committee.

Information is needed about four sets of expectations: (1) expectations for new students, (2) expectations for returning students, (3) faculty expectations of student performance in the settings for which they are primarily responsible (for example, classroom, laboratory, studio), and (4) student affairs expectations of students outside those academic venues. Expectations of other stakeholders, such as trustees, parents and family members, and food service or physical plant staff, might also be of interest. Instruments such as the College Student Expectations Questionnaire (which is adapted from the College Student Experiences Questionnaire; Kuh, Vesper, Connolly, and Pace, 1997; Pace, 1990) can be modified to assess the expectations of these different groups across a range of activities.

Students begin to form expectations and assumptions about college life long before they complete an application for admission. When a college or university clearly states what it values and expects, prospective students and their families have information they need to decide whether the institution is a good match for them. Clear statements about "what it means to be a student here" also help students who matriculate decide how to use their time wisely and behave appropriately (Kuh et al., 1991).

But colleges do not always communicate clear, or high, expectations to students. Consider a five-minute presentation by a residence life professional as part of a question-and-answer session for prospective students and family members. After introducing herself and welcoming the group, she said, "The residence halls are a real fun place to live." Then she described a typical room, telling students that they could bring their "TV, VCR, CD player, and all the stuff you need like that . . . and a computer, too" (thank goodness!). She concluded by assuring students that though college life could be demanding, there would "always be time for that 'must see' television show." This well-intentioned staff member was trying to make the residence halls seem an appealing place to live. But in her zeal to please, she overemphasized the social aspects of campus life, understated the important role campus residences play in the academic mission of the university, and sent the wrong messages about how students should expect to spend their time.

In contrast, some institutions (Kuh et al., 1991) go to great lengths during recruitment, summer orientation and registration, and fall welcome week to ensure that new students receive accurate messages about what the institution expects of them, inside and outside the classroom. For example, the New Undergraduate Student Information Project at Stanford University coordinates the efforts of the campus offices that need to communicate with new students (admissions, orientation, bursar, registrar, housing and residential services, advising) to clearly and consistently articulate institutional expectations (Kuh, 1991a). To underscore the importance of intellectual activity, some colleges and universities (for example, Miami University in Ohio, University of Nebraska-Lincoln) ask incoming students to read articles or books that are then discussed in small groups facilitated by faculty or student affairs staff during fall orientation; a variation of this idea has the author of the required reading give a talk during orientation. During summer orientation and registration, Indiana University faculty members give brief presentations, including tips for analyzing a topic and preparing a persuasive paper or essay examination. These activities have one thing in common: they are designed to emphasize that college is first and foremost about serious intellectual discourse, and to communicate to students that they are expected actively to engage in the intellectual life of the institution.

Step 3. Examine Gaps Between the Expectations the Institution Desires and Those That Are Actually Implemented

The primary goal of this step is to identify discrepancies between the revised institutional expectations (see Step 1) and what students experience and how students behave. Process indicators are one measure of student performance that can be used to see whether the expectations of students and the institution are being realized (Kuh, Vesper, and Pace, 1997). Locally designed or national standardized instruments such as the College Student Experiences Questionnaire (Pace, 1990) can be used to determine the extent to which students engage in activities that research shows make a positive contribution to learning and personal development. The following list is illustrative of common out-of-class activities that have been linked to desired outcomes of college (Kuh, Branch Douglas, et al., 1994; Pascarella and Terenzini, 1991):

- Attending cultural events on campus and in the local community

- Talking with faculty about assignments and career plans

- Discussing academic program matters with advisers

- Working with other students on class-related projects or community service initiatives

- Attending talks by visiting experts in the union or other settings

- Talking with other students about campus issues, new ideas and views of people, or major social issues

- Working on campus committees

- Making friends with students from different groups, including from different racial or ethnic backgrounds

- Using information from classes or reading in conversations with others or applying such information to one's job

Student culture is another area that warrants attention when evaluating student behavior in light of the institution's enhanced performance expectations. At some institutions, the norms and mores that students themselves have established over time inhibit their meeting institutional expectations. As a result, for example, a few weeks into the first semester new students study fewer hours than they thought they would prior to coming to college. The student culture teaches newcomers how to get by with less. Many institutions are coconspirators in this effort, as they herd new students into large, introductory classes that employ few activities to involve students during and after class and require little personal accountability for performance.

Step 4. Develop Strategies for Addressing Gaps Between Desired Institutional Expectations and Student Performance

Some institutional policies and practices will probably have to be modified to ensure that student behavior and experiences are consistent with institutional expectations. Some faculty members might have unreasonably high expectations for student performance, given students' background and abilities, and do little to support and encourage students to use the institution's resources to acquire the skills needed to perform at an acceptable level. Other faculty members and student affairs professionals might say they have high expectations for their students but fail to hold them accountable for behavior that falls consistently short of what is expected, such as letting unexcused absences pass without comment or consequence.

Consistent and clear feedback is necessary for connecting institutional expectations to student performance. There is a great deal of evidence that the more students study, the more they learn (Pace, 1990). Student affairs professionals at residential campuses are well positioned to observe the amount of time and effort students spend studying and the extent to which residential environments are conducive to effective academic achievement. Because of their proximity to students in informal settings, these staff members can let students know whether they are devoting enough time and energy to the activities that matter for learning and personal development.

Reinforcing institutional expectations for students requires that student affairs professionals, as well as faculty members and academic administrators, take the time to review the quality of students' participation and be skillful at giving students feedback. If students are asked to, and do, get more involved in educationally purposeful activities, and read more and write more, faculty and staff might have to spend more time evaluating students' work. Faculty and staff will also have to be available when students seek help, frequently at hours and places at odds with faculty and staff preferences. All this means a significant amount of additional individual and institutional effort. Indeed, faculty and student affairs staff who raise their expectations for student performance and hold students to high standards risk the disapproval of their colleagues who cannot or do not want to work harder.

Two caveats apply when planning institutional action to reduce the gap between the student performance and institutional expectations. First, the messages sent to students should be analyzed periodically to make certain that institutional expectations and promises are not too far ahead of students' experiences, lest students decide that the institution differs too much from what was described to them. If students' experiences do not match what they were led by institutional agents to expect, the consequences can include frustration, poor performance, and, in some instances, premature student departure (Tinto, 1993). High expectations also can exacerbate stress, which mental health professionals say is already at unusually high levels among undergraduate students. Equally troublesome, unrealistic expectations sometimes force students into acts of academic dishonesty, alcohol or drug abuse, or unhealthy eating habits.

Second, some institutions are content to communicate expectations through detailed student conduct codes. Although such documents can provide legal protection for the university and protect due process rights for students, they can inadvertently "allow students to abdicate responsibility . . . [because the rules] may be seen by students as something for which they have no ownership" (Kuh et al., 1991, p. 327). Student conduct codes can also have the unintended effect of preempting discussion about what constitutes appropriate behavior in an academic community, thus effectively precluding students from examining existing community standards and their individual roles and responsibilities for contributing to the welfare of others. Moreover, such documents tend to focus on what is unacceptable, rather than challenge students to conduct themselves in ways that exceed their own expectations.

Step 5. Cultivate an Ethos of Learning

Expectations are inextricably tied to beliefs. An ethos of learning (Kuh, 1993b) is a belief system widely shared among faculty, student affairs professionals, academic administrators, and others that guides transactions between institutions and students. This belief system features a holistic philosophy of learning that acknowledges the mutually shaping relationship between in-class and out-of-class experiences and an assumption that all students can and will meet the high expectations that faculty and student affairs professionals have for their performance. The latter sentiment is eloquently summarized in the credo of noted educator, J. Herman Blake: "There is no known limit to the capacity of the human mind to learn, grow, develop, and change" (personal communication, December 2, 1997).

An ethos of learning has three additional components that complement high expectations. First is an ethic of care (Kuh et al., 1991). Students can tell when their teachers do not think well of them or their abilities. Many students at the margins—however defined—give up when they sense that they do not "matter" to the people around them (Kuh, 1997b). Hence, they do not have an opportunity to elevate their performance to meet the institution's expectations and thereby miss out on the benefits of exceeding their own.

Institutions with an ethos of learning also are marked by an ethic of membership (Kuh et al., 1991). These colleges and universities tell students when they arrive that they are full members of the institution with all rights and privileges; students are also told that they will succeed and graduate, and they are taught how to take advantage of the institution's resources for learning. Such learning environments simultaneously empower and challenge students to perform at high levels, and differ markedly from, for example, a university where instructors of introductory engineering courses declare to their academically able students that at least half of them will not be permitted to take subsequent engineering courses and will need either to transfer or select another major.

The third characteristic of an ethos of learning is a culture of collaboration rooted in good practices in undergraduate education (Education Commission of the States, 1995) and student affairs (as described in this book). Such a culture rarely emerges in the natural course of events; it must be intentionally stitched into an institution's fabric through celebratory events, intentional recruitment and socialization activities, on-going professional development events open to all, and collaborative efforts throughout the institution. Collaboration is essential if, as mentioned earlier, student affairs professionals, faculty members, and academic administrators are to send consistent messages about what they and the institution expect of students. Only through collaboration can faculty and staff learn about the rich array of learning opportunities that exist, develop a common language, and establish working relationships. This is especially important for helping faculty members understand and appreciate how out-of-class experiences on and off the campus contribute to realizing the institution's educational objectives (Kuh, Branch Douglas, et al., 1994).

> The campus' dormitories, cafeterias, student clubs, fraternities, sororities, student organizations, and athletic teams are all places of education, willy-nilly or by design. It is in those arenas that perhaps the most important of the goals intended to be achieved by curricular means can be most effectively furthered—though surely not

with ease and surely not by means of regulations prohibiting this or requiring that, but by the building of an
ethos that is, as befits institutions of higher education,
ahead of the society that surrounds them. [Weingartner,
1994, p. 19]

Conclusion

Students are more likely to perform at high levels when expectations for their behavior are clearly stated and set at the highest appropriate level, given their background and abilities. Unfortunately,
as reported earlier, data from various sources (Kuh, Vesper, and Pace,
1997; Sax et al., 1995, 1996) suggest a disappointing pattern of discrepancies between what faculty and staff say they expect from students and what students do in college. For this reason, it has never
been more important to set high expectations for students. To have
the desired effect, however, high expectations for student and institutional performance must be buttressed by other good practices
in undergraduate education (feedback, respect for diverse learning
approaches).

Because many more students are capable of achieving more than
they imagine, it is incumbent on student affairs professionals and
their faculty colleagues to nurture, cajole, and challenge students
to think bigger thoughts, set higher goals for their learning and personal development, and accomplish more for themselves, their families, and their communities. Indeed, it is almost certain that if
institutions do not expect more from students than students expect
of themselves, the most precious of resources will be wasted—the
resource of human potential.

5

Using Systematic Inquiry to Improve Performance

Ernest T. Pascarella and Elizabeth J. Whitt

Good practice in student affairs occurs when student affairs educators ask, "What are students learning from our programs and services, and how can their learning be enhanced?" Knowledge of and ability to analyze research about students and their learning are critical components of good student affairs practice. Student affairs educators who are skilled in using research and assessment methods acquire high-quality information; effective application of this information to practice results in programs and change strategies that improve institutional and student achievement [ACPA and NASPA, 1997, p. 4].

Scene One: The peer alcohol educators (PAE) at Northwest College are involved in a workshop on crisis management. At the end of today's session, the workshop facilitator asks the PAE to "write a one-minute paper; tell me what was the most important thing you learned today, and what questions you still have on this topic."

Scene Two: The director of commuter student services at Metro University is holding a focus group interview with six commuting students, one of four focus groups she talks with each semester. She opens this interview as she opens all of them, by asking, "What have you learned this month, or this semester, and how have you learned it? What is the best thing that has happened to you since our last interview? What could be going better for you?"

Scene Three: Rosedale College's associate dean for residential education has set aside one hour in his weekly meetings with the hall directors to talk about research and writing on college students, their learning, and organizational effectiveness in student affairs. The directors take turns leading discussions on journal articles, books, and monographs, including brainstorming about how the information can be used in Rosedale's residence halls. Today's session focuses on research on the impact of living-learning communities on first-year student learning outcomes.

Scene Four: The vice chancellor for student affairs and the provost at New State University (NSU) are meeting with the NSU board of governors to announce an important new initiative. They, and representatives from both their divisions, have developed a joint project to study student learning—inside and outside the classroom—at NSU. All students will take achievement tests, complete questionnaires about their experiences, and participate in interviews about their lives and learning at the beginning and end of every year they attend NSU. The research has been designed by a team of faculty and student affairs staff and will be conducted by the newly organized NSU Office of Student Affairs Research.

What do these scenes have in common? Each illustrates the use of systematic inquiry in student affairs. The examples, as a group, introduce two points underscored throughout this chapter: (1) systematic inquiry takes many forms, from simple to complex, and can occur anywhere in an organization, and (2) systematic inquiry is a necessary element of the daily lives of all student affairs professionals. Student affairs work can be conducted without systematic inquiry but, we would argue, it is foolhardy to do so.

The purpose of this chapter is to examine the role of systematic inquiry in good student affairs practice. We begin with a definition of systematic inquiry and a description of several of its forms. A discussion of the relevance and importance of systematic inquiry to student affairs effectiveness follows. The chapter concludes with implications of this principle for student affairs, including potential obstacles to systematic inquiry and suggestions for putting the principle into practice.

Defining and Describing the Principle

What do we mean by *systematic inquiry*? According to the Funk and Wagnalls Standard College Dictionary (1966) et al., *systematic* means methodical, painstaking, intentional, well-ordered, and "carried out with organized regularity." *Inquiry* is (1) the process of seeking information or knowledge, and (2) investigating by asking questions. Therefore, systematic inquiry, for our purposes, is an intentional, organized, and ongoing search for information.

Defining *Systematic Inquiry* in Action

This definition connotes the use of inquiry methods that strive for maximum dependability and accuracy of the information obtained. Persons who conduct quantitative research are likely to use terms such as *reliability* and *validity* to capture the notions of dependability and accuracy (Light, Singer, and Willett, 1990). Researchers who use qualitative research methods concern themselves with trustworthiness of their data and their results (Lincoln and Guba, 1985; Whitt, 1991). In both cases, the concern is whether the results of the inquiry can be believed, for if the inquiry is to be useful, the results must be believable. Our definition of systematic inquiry, then, includes the requirement that the information collected be valid, reliable, and believable.

The phrase *systematic inquiry* calls to mind at least three forms of methodical information-seeking relevant to student affairs professionals: research, assessment, and evaluation. Some writers have clearly differentiated these processes. For example, Upcraft and Schuh (1996), in their book on assessment in student affairs, stated that "assessment guides good practice [and] research guides theory and conceptual foundations" (p. 21); evaluation, according to

Upcraft and Schuh, is the use of assessment data to improve effectiveness. Similarly, Erwin (1996) defined assessment as a form of evaluation that is concerned with "defining, measuring, collecting, analyzing, and using information to enrich the educational experience" at a particular institution, whereas research focuses on "advancing the professional knowledge of the higher education community [by] forming new theories [and] confirming or refuting existing theories" (p. 417).

Other authors do not make such distinctions. Beeler and Hunter (1991) defined *student affairs research* as the collection and use of "reliable information about students and their experiences, about the campus environment, [and] about program effectiveness to support . . . planning and programming decisions" (pp. 7, 8). Light, Singer, and Willet (1990) used the term *research* to refer to "systematic ways to use information to improve teaching and learning" (p. 2). In these definitions, research is not a scholarly activity removed from notions of institutional effectiveness and good practice but, rather, is essential to them. From this perspective, research, assessment, and evaluation are presumed to serve common purposes and involve similar approaches, so treating them as distinct activities is not particularly useful. We have chosen the latter approach in this chapter and so use *systematic inquiry* to encompass research, assessment, and evaluation processes.

Describing Systematic Inquiry in Practice

Good student affairs practice requires systematic inquiry regarding students and their learning. These efforts are focused on collecting and analyzing information both outside and inside the college or university or student affairs organization, and using that information in policymaking, planning, and decision making.

First, systematic inquiry is examining, understanding, and applying the extensive body of research and scholarship about college outcomes and learning environments. What do student affairs practitioners, as a field, know about students and how they are influenced by college? What conditions, experiences, and environments foster desired student outcomes? In what ways does student affairs contribute to those outcomes? Knowledge about these and other topics is growing rapidly (for example, Astin, 1993; Baxter Magolda, 1992; Chickering and Reisser, 1993; Kuh, Schuh, Whitt, and Associates, 1991; Pascarella, Edison, Whitt, Nora, Hagedorn, and Terenzini, 1996; Pascarella and Terenzini, 1991; Pascarella, Whitt, Nora, Edison, Hagedorn, and Terenzini, 1996), and there simply is no excuse for student affairs practitioners to be ignorant of its existence or to formulate programs and policies as though it did not exist.

Much of this literature focuses on the intellectual and developmental influences of student experiences that fall directly or indirectly in the purview of student affairs. For example, research on multi-institutional samples of students highlights the importance of out-of-class experiences and interactions with peers as salient influences on affective and cognitive growth during college (for example, Kuh, 1993b, 1995; Pascarella, Whitt et al., 1996; Terenzini, Pascarella, and Blimling, 1996; Whitt, Edison, Pascarella, Nora, and Terenzini, 1997). In addition, recent results from the Cooperative Institutional Research Program and the federally funded National Study of Student Learning provide new information on how aspects of student life such as Greek affiliation, service learning, involvement in extracurricular activities, athletic participation, work and work-study programs, and institutional climate influence a wide range of college outcomes (Astin, 1993, 1996; Pascarella, Bohr, Nora, and Terenzini, 1995a, 1995b; Pascarella, Edison et al., 1996; Pascarella, Edison, Nora, Hagedorn, and Terenzini, 1996; Pascarella, Edison, Nora, Hagedorn, and Terenzini, 1998; Pascarella, Whitt, Edison, Nora, Hagedorn, Yeager, and Terenzini, 1997; Terenzini, Springer, Pascarella, and Nora, 1995a, 1995b). Good practice in student affairs requires becoming familiar with these and other relevant studies and using the information they provide to inform development of plans, policies, and programs.

Second, systematic inquiry also means making effective use of institutional research activities. Who are your students? What do your students learn and where do they learn it? Do different groups of students differ in learning outcomes and, if so, why? Offices of institutional research typically collect data and produce reports that provide up-to-date information about, among other things, students and their progress, student retention and degree completion, and graduates' perceptions of institutional impact. When employed judiciously, these can provide valuable contextual information for student affairs activities such as strategic planning.

Systematic inquiry within an institution goes beyond using data from an office of institutional research, however. Perhaps more than any other constituency on campus, student affairs is concerned with the quality of all aspects of students' lives and the impact of the total educational experience on students (Astin, 1996; Kuh, Branch Douglas, et al., 1994; Levine, 1994; Pascarella, 1997; Terenzini et al., 1996). A clear understanding of how (not just what) aspects of the institution contribute to or inhibit student learning and development is necessary. Acquiring this understanding requires that student affairs practitioners be willing and able to develop and implement a comprehensive and systematic program of inquiry about students and their learning.

Third, good practice requires systematic inquiry about student affairs programs, practices, policies, and services. What is the impact of your services on student learning? In what ways do student affairs policies and programs contribute to the educational mission of the institution? If, for example, student affairs staff in residence life and campus activities are required to engage in educational programming, what, if any, evidence demonstrates that such programs result in desired learning outcomes? Offering such programs as opportunities from which learning is assumed to occur, or because past participants said they were useful, is increasingly risky in the current climate of accountability (Stimpson, 1994; Whitt, 1996b; Whitt and Associates, in press), a topic to which we turn next.

Warrant for Systematic Inquiry in Student Affairs

Systematic inquiry is an essential aspect of good student affairs practice for many reasons; chief among these is the significant role inquiry plays in effective institutional and student performance. Perhaps the most persuasive argument for using systematic inquiry in all aspects of student affairs, however, is that it is an effective response to the demands for accountability in today's colleges and universities. Each of these warrants for inquiry—effectiveness and survival—is discussed in the following sections.

Systematic Inquiry for Effective Performance

There is a great deal of evidence linking research, assessment, and evaluation activities to desired student outcomes outside the classroom (for example, Astin, 1991, 1993, 1996; Benedict, 1991; Kuh, 1996a; Kuh et al., 1991; Kuh, Branch Douglas, et al., 1994; Light et al., 1990; Pike, Schroeder, and Berry, 1997; Terenzini et al., 1996; Upcraft and Schuh, 1996). For example, in their review of research on out-of-class learning, Kuh, Branch Douglas, et al. (1994) concluded that systematic assessment of institutional programs, policies, and practices, as well as student performance, is one of the conditions associated with fostering student involvement "in educationally purposeful out-of-class activities" (p. 47). These researchers, and others, note the importance of collecting accurate and timely data about students, their learning, and the environments that influence that learning, including student affairs programs, policies, services, and practices. Research from other settings about student learning outcomes and the role of out-of-class experiences in that learning can help interpret and elicit meaning from those data and suggest other research to pursue or practices to adapt. Equally important is the use of the data in making decisions about planning, policymaking, problem solving, and allocation of resources. Systematic inquiry serves little purpose unless the information it provides is put to good use (Kinnick, 1985).

Systematic inquiry is a key element in learning organizations, a popular topic in recent research and writing about productivity in the corporate world (Brown, 1997; Garvin, 1993; Kuh, 1996a; Senge, 1990a). Learning organizations obtain, create, and transfer knowledge and change their behavior on the basis of that knowledge and the insights it develops (Garvin, 1993). The "building blocks" (Garvin, 1993, p. 81) of learning organizations are five activities: systematic problem solving, experimenting, learning from experiences within the organization, learning from experiences and best practices outside the organization, and transmitting knowledge efficiently and in a timely fashion throughout the organization. All of these activities involve a systematic search for information and use of that information to improve productivity. People who work in learning organizations "must continually ask, 'How do we know that's true?' . . . They must push beyond obvious symptoms to assess underlying causes, often collecting evidence when conventional wisdom says it is unnecessary" (Garvin, 1993, p. 82).

Although the notion of a *learning organization* seems a good fit with the purposes and processes of higher education (where, for example, we might expect to find many people in the habit of asking "How do we know that's true?"), it has only recently been applied to colleges and universities (Brown, 1997; Kuh, 1996a; Tinto, 1997). In an article on organizational learning in *About Campus,* Judy Brown (1997) posed the question, "How might student affairs departments and divisions embody organizational learning?" (p. 6). Among many answers to that question, she offered the following: "We would take seriously the liberal arts idea of the continual, rigorous, and unblaming examination of all ideas. . . . It would require that we use the habit of mind of both science and the humanities in our study of the student experience. We would attend to both data and belief, measurement and metaphor" (p. 10).

The student affairs division as learning organization embodies and embraces what Robert Brown (1991) has referred to as "an ethos of inquiry" (p. 125). An ethos of inquiry is characterized by commitments to look for explanations for what occurs (or does not occur) in data and other evidence in one's own setting, to examine research and practice from other sources and settings, and to improve current practice by using those data. In the learning organization, an essential role for student affairs professionals is the inquirer who systematically engages in reflection and study regarding students and their learning and student affairs processes and practices (Kuh, 1996a). By approaching their work in this way, student affairs professionals will not only help foster effective environments and experiences for learning, they will model the critical thinking, analysis, and decision-making skills they desire for students (American College Personnel Association [ACPA], 1994; Haworth, 1997).

Although creating and maintaining student affairs organizations that foster student learning and achievement of the institution's educational mission might seem to be the sine qua non of student affairs practice, it is not enough in today's colleges and universities. Student affairs also must demonstrate that effectiveness to others within and outside their institutions. Systematic inquiry assists in that endeavor as well.

Systematic Inquiry for Survival

In Chapter One, Gregory Blimling and Elizabeth Whitt describe the clamor in the past decade to restructure and refocus postsecondary education in the United States to control costs, improve quality, and increase productivity. Most higher education reformers believe that the most effective means for colleges and universities to achieve these goals is to focus resources and energy on student learning (National Association of State Universities and Land-Grant Colleges [NASULGC], 1997; Study Group on Conditions of Excellence in Higher Education [Study Group], 1984; Wingspread Group, 1993a).

Accompanying this interest in student learning are calls to demonstrate that (1) learning does, indeed, occur in our institutions of higher education and (2) the institutions' people, programs, and curricula contribute to that learning (NASULGC, 1997; Study Group, 1984; Wingspread Group, 1993). The Wingspread Group's report, for example, asserted that "putting learning at the heart of the enterprise means campuses must . . . systematically apply the very best of what is known about learning and teaching on their campuses [and] rigorously assess what their students know and are able to do in order to improve both student and institutional performance" (p. 13). In other words, "a quality education is one in which the student learns—and you had better have the evidence!" (Hanson, 1991, p. 81).

All indications are that the pressure on colleges and universities to prove higher education does what it claims to do, and does so efficiently and effectively, is here to stay (Banta and Associates, 1993; Banta, Lund, Black, and Oblander, 1996; Guskin, 1994a, 1994b; Terenzini, 1989; Upcraft and Schuh, 1996). Also, all signs point to the fact that programs, services, and activities that fail to implement effective assessment processes or fail to demonstrate specific contributions to the educational mission of the institution are in peril (Guskin, 1994a, 1994b; Terenzini, 1989; Upcraft and Schuh, 1996).

Although the press for assessment and accountability affects all aspects of a college or university, there is some evidence that student affairs is particularly vulnerable. For example, in his 1994 *Change* article on improving administrative productivity in higher education, Alan Guskin made the following assertion: "Strategically, enhancing student learning and reducing student costs are, in my judgment, the primary yardstick [for organizational effectiveness]. *Since the faculty and academic areas are most directly tied to student learning, alterations in the lower priority support areas must precede* [major changes in the role of the faculty] [emphasis added]" (p. 29).

We do not quote Guskin to resurrect the specter of second-class citizenship for student affairs—may that conversation rest in peace (Allen and Garb, 1993)—or to blame the faculty for student affairs' vulnerability. His statement is, instead, one view—probably not unique to Mr. Guskin—of what happens when student learning is the measure of institutional productivity: The aspects of the university that are most clearly associated with student learning have priority for funding and for surviving reductions in funding and personnel (ACPA, 1994; Guskin, 1994a, 1994b). Because "there is no presumption that out-of-class activities result in student learning consistent with educational goals" (Blimling and Alschuler, 1996, p. 214), student affairs work can, indeed, be viewed as "a lower priority support area." And so, by implication, Guskin's statement reflects what happens if student affairs organizations cannot demonstrate that their programs, services, and people are an integral aspect of student learning.

Under these circumstances, systematic inquiry is not just a means to effectiveness but is essential to survival (Hanson, 1991; Upcraft and Schuh, 1996). Without research and assessment, "student affairs is left only to logic, intuition, moral imperatives, good will, or serendipity in justifying its existence" (Upcraft and Schuh, 1996, p. 12). None of those tactics seems a good idea for the long run.

Yet many student affairs practitioners cling to these and other traditional tactics for justifying their existence rather than embrace systematic inquiry as a more effective alternative (Beeler and Hunter, 1991; Blimling and Alschuler, 1996; Kalsbeek, 1994; Upcraft and Schuh, 1996). For example, student affairs divisions and professionals have been slow to get involved in rigorous assessment of student learning outside the classroom (Brown, 1991; Erwin, 1991; Upcraft and Schuh, 1996). This has been easy to do because, for a variety of reasons, much of the assessment movement in higher education has focused on student learning inside the classroom and on academic outcomes (Banta et al., 1996; Ewell, 1985; RiCharde, Olney, and Erwin, 1993). In the absence of documented evidence of student affairs' contributions to student learning, however, those contributions are likely to be ignored or, at best, underestimated (Blimling and Alschuler, 1996)—good reasons to press for a significant role in institutional assessment plans, whether invited or not.

Student affairs practitioners' reluctance to treat systematic inquiry as a taken-for-granted professional activity will be addressed in more detail in the following section. Suffice it to say here, by way of summary, that the evidence is clear. Systematic inquiry—in the form of research, assessment, and evaluation—is absolutely necessary, not only for maximum effectiveness in achieving organizational and individual goals, but also for maintaining a key role for student affairs divisions in achieving the educational mission of their institutions (ACPA, 1994).

Implications of the Principle for Student Affairs Practice

In this section we identify helping and restraining forces within student affairs that can affect the extent to which systematic inquiry is, and can be, implemented on a broad scale. We also describe some resources available to student affairs professionals for undertaking systematic inquiry.

Student Affairs and Systematic Inquiry: Some Bad News

In 1938, Esther Lloyd-Jones and Margaret Smith proclaimed that "student personnel work is now at the stage where basic studies can and must be made if we in this field are not to be content to be merely counters and arrangers of the obvious" (p. 283). Yet sixty years later, concerns abound that student affairs research and student affairs professionals have not fulfilled this early promise. To the contrary, many involved in student affairs (for example, Benedict, 1991; Blimling and Alschuler, 1996; Brown, 1991; Erwin, 1991, 1996; Hanson, 1991) question the extent to which student affairs practitioners, in general, are committed to systematic inquiry in any form.

Calls to integrate research and assessment into student affairs practice have been characterized as "about as realistic as . . . saving the Brazilian rain forest [or] achieving world peace. Everyone is talking about it, but not many people are doing much about it" (Benedict, 1991, pp. 18–19). One can argue that there is a large gap between what student affairs practitioners say about the value and importance of research and assessment to their work and the extent to which such activities are actually conducted and used. Systematic inquiry is "the missing ingredient" (Erwin, 1996, p. 416) in much student affairs practice.

If systematic inquiry in all its forms is essential not only to student affairs effectiveness, but also to student affairs survival, why is it a "missing ingredient"? Several explanations have been offered, most of which focus on student affairs professionals themselves and the nature of their work and training (for example, Beeler and Hunter, 1991; Benedict, 1991; Brown, 1991; Erwin, 1991, 1996; Hanson, 1991; Kuh, Bean, Bradley, and Coomes, 1986). In their excellent monograph on student affairs research, Karl Beeler and Deborah Hunter (1991) posited that "somewhere between its theoretical promise and its actual practice, student affairs research falls prey to anxiety, busy schedules, and reactionary management" (p. viii). In other words, many student affairs professionals believe that research-related activities are too difficult, and require too much time, to be practical (Benedict, 1991). Others believe systematic inquiry is too expensive to be a priority and is, instead, a "frill" (Brown, 1986, p. 195). Still others fear that they do not have the skills to use, or conduct, research effectively and so avoid it altogether (Beeler and Hunter, 1991; Benedict, 1991).

Leaders of student affairs divisions and units have been described as a particular obstacle to the use of student affairs research because they do not model commitment to systematic inquiry (Brown, 1991; Kuh et al., 1986). Evidence of this can be found in failure to demand that decisions, policies, and programs reflect the best, most recent, data available; claims from student affairs administrators that they do not have time to keep up with the knowledge base in the field or to implement research themselves; or assertions that the nature of student affairs work (for example, difficult-to-measure constructs of student development) does not lend itself to assessment

(Blimling and Alschuler, 1996; Erwin, 1991, 1996; Hanson, 1991; Kuh et al., 1986).

Other explanations for inadequate systematic inquiry in student affairs focus on student affairs and higher education research. Research conducted by higher education scholars and published in higher education and social science journals has been characterized as too complicated, too narrowly focused, and too concerned with sophisticated quantitative methods to have any policy or practical relevance (Brown, 1991; Keller, 1985; Kinnick, 1985; Terenzini, Pascarella, and Blimling, 1996). Publication in scholarly journals is an important criterion for promotion and tenure at research universities, but such venues are not necessarily designed to provide research in clear and accessible language useful for formulating policy. Indeed, "the language of research can be arcane, obscure, and unintelligible to ordinary mortals" (Benedict, 1991, p. 21). Concerns also have been expressed about the usefulness of student affairs research that is atheoretical, what Robert Brown (1991) called the "'I-was-walking-on-campus-one-day' or 'I-was-wondering-what-if' research" (p. 128).

Ultimately, explanations or excuses for not doing, or using, research in student affairs matter little in the face of demands that student affairs divisions demonstrate their effectiveness and their contributions to student learning. For student affairs divisions and units, "research is not a frill. Research is a necessity and an obligation" (Brown, 1986, p. 195). What *is* important, therefore, is taking steps to make sure that systematic inquiry is an integral and valued part of any student affairs operation.

Student Affairs and Systematic Inquiry: Some Good News

Now the good news. One piece of good news is that in higher education research in general, and in a growing number of colleges and universities, student learning increasingly is defined to include outcomes that can be achieved outside the classroom and in nonacademic endeavors (American Association for Higher Education

[AAHE], 1992; ACPA, 1994; Banta et al., 1996; Kalsbeek, 1994; Kuh et al., 1991). For example, in the widely disseminated document *Principles of Good Practice for Assessing Student Learning* (AAHE, 1992), the second principle states: "Assessment is most effective when it reflects an understanding of learning as multidimensional [and] integrated. . . . [Learning] entails not only what students know, but what they can do with what they know . . . [and] habits of mind that affect both academic success and performance beyond the classroom" (p. 2). Student affairs professionals have an opportunity to make sure that experiences and learning outside the classroom are included in institutional definitions of learning outcomes and in institutional assessment (Kalsbeek, 1994).

We also see good news in the growing body of evidence that out-of-class experiences play a significant role in the outcomes of college. The long list of studies we provided at the beginning of this chapter is just a sample of what is available to student affairs professionals. A good place to begin to review and use this research is in syntheses of research on student learning (for example, Astin, 1993; Pascarella and Terenzini, 1991), including those that specifically examine the effects of out-of-class experiences and environments (for example, Kuh, Branch Douglas, et al. , 1994; Terenzini et al., 1996). Unfortunately, direct evidence of student affairs staff members' influence on student learning is very limited (Terenzini et al., 1996); this could be good news, however, for persons looking for research topics. In any case, this is a knowledge base ripe for use in designing institutional and student affairs studies and in planning, policymaking, and decision making.

Good news for the field as a whole and for good practice at several institutions in particular is that some universities have created research units within their student affairs divisions and/or have integrated student affairs goals and concerns into institutional research and assessment activities. Examples include University of Missouri-Columbia (cf., Pike, Schroeder, and Berry, 1997), University of Massachusetts at Amherst (cf., Malaney, 1993; Weitzer and Malaney, 1991), Appalachian State University, and James Madison University (cf., RiCharde, Olney, and Erwin, 1993). At James Madison University, for example, both cognitive and affective changes are followed during students' first two years of college (RiCharde, Olney, and Erwin, 1995). Student affairs and academic affairs staff at Appalachian State have designed a program of tests, surveys, and interviews to track student learning inside and outside the classroom across four years of college; the study will be implemented by researchers from outside the institution. These and similar research units and projects offer examples of systematic inquiry in student affairs that can be adapted to other colleges and universities.

The growing recognition that systematic inquiry need not be limited to quantitative studies, and the growing appreciation for the use of qualitative methods in student affairs research also are good news. This is not to say that qualitative methods should take the place of quantitative methods, or that qualitative research should be used to avoid the challenges of designing and implementing quantitative studies (Brown, 1991; Pascarella and Terenzini, 1991; Whitt, 1991). Qualitative methods do, however, offer an effective complement to quantitative research for studying students and their experiences, as well as the processes and outcomes of student affairs work (for example, Kuh and Andreas, 1991; Kuh et al., 1991; Love, 1995).

Collecting data by talking, listening, and observing gives the inquirer an up-close and textured view of many aspects of work and life in college heretofore examined mostly through surveys and questionnaires. Qualitative studies can, for example, provide a detailed look at peer cultures and their influence on learning (for example, Baxter Magolda, 1997; Rhoads, 1995a, 1995b; Stombler and Martin, 1994; Whitt, 1994b). Qualitative research also has been used to focus attention on the experiences of students whose voices can be muffled by traditional studies of college outcomes (for example, Rendon, 1996; Rhoads, 1994; Whitt, 1994a). Qualitative methods can be used to study student learning across institutions (for example, Kuh et al., 1991; Kuh, 1993; Whitt, 1994b), or within a single institution (for example, Baxter Magolda, 1997), at a single point in time (for example, Romano, 1996), or over many years (for example, Baxter Magolda, 1992). In addition, qualitative methods have achieved credibility for conducting assessments of learning outcomes (for example, Upcraft and Schuh, 1996; Whitt, 1996a). Perhaps most important, qualitative studies offer students an opportunity to tell their own stories of life and learning (Baxter Magolda, 1997; Williams, 1997). "Students seldom have the opportunity to tell their stories . . . [yet] students telling stories benefits both the students and those wishing to learn more about them" (Baxter Magolda, 1997, p. 22).

Recent research and writing on classroom assessment techniques also can be useful to student affairs practitioners (Angelo and Cross, 1993). Many of these techniques are simple to use and can readily be adapted to student affairs settings and activities. The "one-minute paper" mentioned in the introduction to this chapter is one example (Angelo and Cross, 1993); this exercise, intended to help teachers and facilitators determine whether students are learning what they think they are teaching, can be used in educational programs, training sessions, and workshops.

Finally, good news for student affairs professionals is that there are many written resources available to assist in undertaking, or sustaining, systematic inquiry. These resources are too numerous to identify here; a few good examples must suffice. Several recent books offer particularly detailed techniques and approaches to assessing student learning outcomes, including outside the classroom (for example, Angelo and Cross, 1993; Banta and Associates, 1993; Banta et al., 1996; Kuh, 1990; Kuh, 1993a; Kuh et al., 1991; Stage, 1992; Upcraft and Schuh, 1996). Useful frameworks and descriptions of student affairs research units, as well as possible research agendas, also are available (for example, Beeler and Hunter, 1991; Brown, 1991; Kuh et al., 1991; Kuh, Branch Douglas, et al., 1994; Malaney, 1993; Malaney and Weitzer, 1993; Pascarella and Terenzini, 1998;

Weitzer and Malaney, 1991). Instruments for studying students and their learning outside the classroom include the College Student Experience Questionnaire (for example, Kuh et al., 1994), the Community College Student Experience Questionnaire (for example, Friedlander, Murrell, and MacDougall, 1993), and the Involving College Audit Protocol (Kuh et al., 1991). The reference list for this chapter also could serve as a place to begin one's search for information about systematic inquiry in student affairs.

Putting the Principle into Practice: Recommendations for Systematic Inquiry in Student Affairs

We offer the following recommendations for undertaking systematic inquiry—in the forms of research, assessment, and evaluation—in student affairs practice. We also provide a modest agenda for persons interested in pursuing local research on students and their learning.

1. *Develop an "ethos of inquiry" within the student affairs organization.* This recommendation includes a commitment to using evidence and information from research in all aspects of practice, including routine decisions, planning processes, problem solving, and policymaking, and integrating systematic inquiry into the daily operations of the student affairs organization. Implementing this recommendation effectively requires a commitment to systematic inquiry on the part of organizational leaders, especially the chief student affairs officer (CSAO). Indeed, "CSAO's are in a position to remodel the entire profession's orientation toward research" (Brown, 1991, p. 135). This also means hiring staff members who are skilled at systematic inquiry and making staff development on inquiry-related topics an expectation.

2. *Commit resources to systematic inquiry.* Include subscriptions to professional journals and an up-to-date library of books on stu-

dents, their learning, and inquiry; time for staff to stay informed about research and writing on student learning; time and money to develop and pursue an agenda of research within the student affairs organization; time and money to pursue small research projects relevant to student affairs goals and priorities; and resources for professional development activities to help staff become effective inquirers. It is likely that committing resources to systematic inquiry will require moving resources away from some other activities. As difficult as this may be to envision, keep in mind the critical connections between research, assessment, and evaluation and organizational effectiveness and survival.

3. *Develop and implement a comprehensive plan for assessment of student learning and the role of student affairs in that learning.* Elements of such a plan should include collaboration among student affairs and academic affairs personnel, and training and development for staff members in research, assessment, and evaluation activities. In addition to rigorous and meaningful evaluations of the effectiveness of student affairs programs, services, policies, and people, an inquiry agenda for a student affairs organization should include some or all of the following:

- How do your students spend their time, and how does that influence college outcomes?

- Who are your students? What are they like, what do they know, and what do they need when they arrive at your institution? What do they gain as a result of being at your institution?

- What do students learn (for example, cognitive, interpersonal, intrapersonal, and practical outcomes) over their time at your college, and how?

- Detailed descriptions of campus learning environments and students' experiences, and descriptions of campus climates (for example, in-class and out-of-class, for students of color, for women; for part-time and/or commuting students) and cultures (for example, student cultures, cultures within student affairs, academic cultures). How do different campus environments and experiences influence different types of students?

- How do off-campus environments and experiences influence learning?

- What do student affairs programs, services, policies, and people contribute to student learning outcomes? Do these activities inhibit learning in any way?

- What are your students' stories about learning, life as a student, their peers, student affairs professionals, about whatever they are thinking about?

- What is the relationship among the institution's educational mission and the policies, programs, and practices of the various student affairs units?

Research at the institutional level on these topics would make an important contribution to student affairs practice as well as to the general body of knowledge about students and their learning. Our last two recommendations follow:

4. *Designate responsibility for student affairs inquiry.* Although systematic inquiry should be a widely shared activity, assigning someone (or some small committee, or an office of student affairs research) responsibility for all aspects of research, assessment, and evaluation for the division can help ensure that they stay on everyone's agenda and everyone's mind. If your organization does not include individuals who have the expertise to implement effective assessment and research efforts, consider hiring someone who does. Establish a research unit within the student affairs division and hire

experts to run that operation, or use outside consultants to get your inquiry started and to keep those efforts going.

5. *Start somewhere.* If comprehensive research agendas and plans are beyond your organization's expertise and hiring assistance is beyond your means, do *something.* Set time aside every week for staff to talk about research and writing on students and how that research could be applied to your setting. Ask students what they are learning and how. Simple questions—such as "What have you learned here?" or "What have you learned this week?" or "What is the most interesting thing you have done this semester?"—can elicit rich and useful responses. An important byproduct of this effort is giving students opportunities to feel heard. Discuss students' answers to these questions and use them in decision making and goal setting. If a division-wide commitment to inquiry is out of the question at the moment, identify and bring together interested individuals to pursue small projects.

Conclusion

The *Student Learning Imperative* (ACPA, 1994) describes a learning-oriented student affairs division as a place where, among other things, staff are experts on students, their learning, and the environments in which learning takes place and where "student affairs policies and programs are based on promising practices from the research on student learning and institution-specific assessment data" (pp. 3–4). Good practice in the form of systematic inquiry is necessary, therefore, to create learning-oriented organizations. More important, perhaps, systematic inquiry is essential to help student affairs practitioners "model what we wish for our students: an ever-increasing capacity for learning and self-reflection" (ACPA, 1994, p. 4).

6

Using Resources to Achieve Institutional Missions and Goals

Linda Reisser and Larry D. Roper

Effective student affairs divisions are responsible stewards of their institutions' financial and human resources. They use principles of organizational planning to create and improve learning environments throughout the campus that emphasize institutions' desired educational outcomes for students. Because the most important resources for learning are human resources, good student affairs divisions involve professionals who can translate into practice guiding theories and research from areas such as human development, learning and cognition, communication, leadership, and program design and implementation [ACPA and NASPA, 1997, p. 4].

The social responsibilities, missions, values, aspirations, and conditions affecting colleges and universities vary greatly. Most have mission statements that address areas such as teaching, research, public service, and relationships with various communities. Some institutions value providing open access, whereas others hold tightly to belief in selectivity in their admissions processes. College and university missions are informed by factors such as church relationship, community charters, land-grant status, the uniqueness of the target population(s) they educate (for example, women's, tribal, historically black, military), their profit/nonprofit focus, and many other variables (Lyons, 1993).

There is probably no institution without a formal mission statement describing its long-term aspirations, core values, and desired educational outcomes for students. Few institutions have static mission statements. They are often rewritten or altered to reflect the institution's growth, changing social conditions, new priorities, or political mandates. Responsible professionals will be well versed in their institution's historical and contemporary missions and have awareness of how they will contribute to its achievement through their leadership.

In addition to the goals they set for themselves, higher education institutions have stakeholders at many levels that expect them to be run in an educationally and socially responsible manner. Among the expectations are fiscal responsibility. Good practice in student affairs work will reflect an awareness of responsibility and accountability to internal and external publics, while showing a firm commitment to the institution's mission. Because the types of higher education institutions vary widely, there is no one prescription for success that can be adopted by student affairs professionals. Professionals on each campus must relate their work to the unique situation of their institution. To accomplish the necessary congruence with the conditions of their campus, student affairs professionals need to develop approaches specific to their own fiscal situation, human resource level, political context, historical legacy, unique mission, and particular social conditions. Such a response requires more than "borrowing" good ideas from other campuses. It demands a high level of creativity, sophisticated problem-solving skills, a willingness and ability to take risks, management and leadership skills, and knowledge. Most important, it will require bold and focused leadership.

The current conditions facing universities and colleges have been widely heralded as among the most challenging in the history of higher education (Ender, Newton, and Caple, 1996; Wingspread Group, 1993). Increasing accountability to the public for educational outcomes, the need to cut costs, reduced funding from external sources, and declining enrollments on some campuses are among the innumerable pressing issues confronting education leaders.

Student affairs professionals are not excluded from the pressures faced by other administrators. They are confronted with issues such as the need to adjust to changing internal and external politics, grapple with the anxiety and change produced by restructuring, reconcile the identity and status differences associated with changes in reporting direction, and increase their contributions to increasingly complex institutions. Although not all campuses are affected by the same concerns and dilemmas, each has its unique issues to which student affairs professionals will need to respond. These broad and emotion-laden challenges require reflective, thoughtful leaders who can promote growth and achievement in student affairs divisions while effectively managing declining human and financial resources.

Student affairs professionals are responsible for using their leadership skills and personal energy to link their professional activities and efforts to the strategic goals and missions of their institutions. This type of leadership is made more difficult by the shifting nature of institutional missions. In the last few years almost two-thirds of universities and colleges surveyed have been engaged in some level of mission, values, or program review, while just over 50 percent have restructured student services units (Kuh, Branch Douglas, Lund, and Ramin-Gyurnik, 1994). As good practice in student affairs work is linked directly to contributing to achievement of the institution's mission and values, changes in mission have necessitated changes in the focus of student affairs. The accompanying restructuring of student affairs programs creates another level of challenge.

These prevailing challenges are being taken seriously by the majority of student affairs professionals, as is evident by the changes in focus by student affairs divisions. Among the most significant changes is the gradual shift in focus to increased emphasis on student development and student learning. Although the concept of student service remains the dominant activity of most student affairs divisions, there is evidence that some campus leaders have enhanced efforts to influence learning outcomes and become more learning-centered. In the situations where these efforts have occurred, more time, energy and financial resources have been shifted in that direction (Ender et al., 1996). Movement in the direction of increasing contributions to student learning is the most profound addition student affairs programs can make to the accomplishment of their institutions' missions. However, success in this arena is not easy to achieve, nor will it be accomplished through traditional planning processes. It requires significant time, planning, dialogue, assessment, and communication with non–student affairs colleagues.

As student affairs professionals strive to achieve the most for their students, they must stay grounded in the practical realities of daily life at colleges and universities. These basic issues center on acting responsibly and being accountable for the leadership and management of human and financial resources. Because many student affairs professionals regard themselves first and foremost as educators, they sometimes commit too little time to understanding effective principles of resource management. Conversely, some student affairs professionals at mid- and senior-level positions come to regard themselves primarily as resource managers and lose sight of the values and principles at the core of their institutional missions. Our situation is unique. We have the dual challenge of being effective, responsible managers while also functioning as inspired, visionary leaders in the achievement of our institutions' missions (Rogers, 1996).

Some leaders have sought to achieve organizational transformation, success, and focus through the use of strategic planning processes. Though such processes can be effective, alone they may be insufficient in environments as complex and fluid as those facing colleges and universities now and in the future. Student affairs leaders need to adopt processes that not only allow them to develop and implement plans to contribute to the institution's future but also support them in protecting the institution's existence. Contemporary leaders must work to ensure a positive future while protecting their institutions from the threats they face today. Good practice in student affairs requires healthy, relevant approaches to the management of institutional well being.

The frequent lament of student affairs professionals about their situation is that they are being "asked to do more with less" (Moneta, 1997). Although such a statement may be descriptive, it may not be accurate. Student affairs professionals have the ability to shape their priorities. The challenge is to accomplish what the institution most needs with the resources available. Good student affairs practice challenges student affairs professionals to establish and prioritize work based on the priority needs of the institution. No matter what level of financial and human resources is allocated to student affairs work on the campus, responsible leadership demands that resources be directed toward achieving outcomes in the areas of greatest institutional need. Leaders must be cognizant of the obstacles that impede success, such as neglecting long-term planning, looking to technology to solve deep-seated organizational problems, looking for examples that can be copied from others, and having too many false starts on important initiatives (Walton, 1986). As they work to change, improve, and transform organizations, student affairs leaders will need to examine unproductive behaviors and thought patterns (Covey, 1990). They will be challenged to break with models that have historically informed student affairs practice and adopt contemporary approaches that respond appropriately to the institutional context in which they are functioning.

Specific leadership initiatives must be implemented to produce the type of focused, outcomes-oriented student affairs work demanded on most campuses. The necessary initiatives cannot be developed in a vacuum, or communicated to staff from on high with the expectation that they will be implemented in a meaningful way. A high level of organizational functioning must be accomplished for good practice to ensue. There is a wide range of theories and philosophies from which professionals may draw in their efforts to meet the dual challenge of managing institutional resources while achieving results consistent with the institution's mission. Among the most prominent tools available are management strategies (Walton, 1986), team building (Bensimon and Neumann, 1993; Dyer, 1995; Larson and LaFasto, 1989), organizational change and development models (Kotter, 1996; Schein, 1992; Senge, 1990a), and leadership theories (Bensimon and Neumann, 1993; Kotter, 1996).

Common Themes Emerging from Theory

Common themes relevant to achieving good practice in student affairs work that are found among available models include the need to understand organizational culture, the necessity for organizations to have an elevating goal or compelling vision, the requirement of good channels of communication, the importance of planning and taking action, the willingness to take risks, an understood sense of urgency, competent employees, and commitment to personal and organizational growth.

Organizational Culture

The organizational cultures of colleges and universities are dynamic. They are constantly evolving environments because of the number and complexity of internal and external factors that influence their functioning (Kuh, 1996a). Schein (1992) describes culture as the pattern of thoughts and behaviors that evolve from the assumptions a group of people learn and pass on to new members. The thoughts, assumptions, and behavior grow from a need to adapt to external circumstances while achieving internal integration. When these approaches work well in solving problems and confronting circumstances, they are validated and passed on to new members as organizationally correct. Over time, a group functioning around common assumptions and like behaviors will create shared values and behavioral norms. These norms and values will persist even when membership changes. When organizations are in need of transformation, the visible (behaviors) and invisible (values) aspects of culture can represent significant obstacles. Of the two cultural dimensions, shared values are more difficult to address because they become ingrained in the belief system of the culture and are not easily replaced (Kotter, 1996).

Culture is the most powerful aspect of an organization and the most difficult aspect to affect. Culture defines what we view as right and wrong, what we classify as important, what we reward and punish, and how we expect others to see the world (Dyer, 1995). Student affairs leaders who want to influence the growth and success of the campus and organization must know the campus culture, how it serves them well and where it impedes them in acting on those issues for which they are accountable. The success of student affairs professionals' achieving good practice will be linked to their ability to influence culture. Affecting the thinking, values, behaviors, and assumptions of those in and out of student affairs represents the first step in being an effective practitioner in higher education.

Elevating Goal or Compelling Vision

A clearly articulated and well-formed vision serves as the basis for promoting institutional growth and establishes anchors for job performance (Dalton, 1996; Rogers, 1996). By developing a vision, student affairs professionals are able to create the groundwork for aligning, directing, and motivating the actions of large numbers of people. One of the primary purposes of a vision is to increase efficiency by providing a common vehicle through which members can view their roles and responsibilities in an organization (Kotter, 1996). The identification of a clear, elevating goal requires student affairs professionals to communicate what is most important in the work they do. A clearly stated goal, linked to the institutional mission, makes known to others the end state toward which the organization aspires. Clarity in a goal provides the foundation for specificity in expectations for groups and individual student affairs professionals (Larson and LaFasto, 1989). An elevating goal or compelling vision will tell those in and out of student affairs what student affairs stands for and what it aspires to contribute to the mission of the institution.

Communication

Most organizations fail to achieve their desired outcomes because of failure to communicate effectively. Too often we undervalue the power of repetition in a message and the incredible impact of leadership behavior that is consistent or inconsistent with espoused ideals (Kotter, 1996). If student affairs programs are to be successful, effective communication systems need to be developed. An important dimension of creating communication systems is the creation of a common language, with special words that have special meaning for members of the organization's culture. A common language increases the likelihood that messages given while doing the work of the university will be understood as they are intended (Schein, 1992).

An effective communication system will have formal and informal dimensions. Among the key characteristics are information that is easily available, credible sources of information, the opportunity for staff members to address issues not on a formal agenda, methods for documenting issues raised and decisions made (Larson and LaFasto, 1989), opportunities for dialogue to enhance learning of members (Senge, 1990a), and processes that allow diverse perspectives represented in the organization to be heard (Kotter, 1996).

Planning and Action

A comprehensive strategic plan can serve as a useful guide in determining whether an institution is fulfilling its expressed mission. At the same time, in the absence of planning it is unlikely that the institutional mission will be achieved. Key elements of effective planning are clarity of purpose, stated goals that relate to institutional purposes, prioritizing of goals, long-term and short-term measurable outcomes, awareness of necessary and available resources to achieve success, specified action steps, assigned responsibilities, and evaluation of programs and personnel (Ern, 1993).

Effective planning and follow-through reinforce the value of using time well, prioritizing for groups and individuals, managing multiple tasks at any given time, and meeting deadlines (Larson and LaFasto, 1989). In the absence of action, planning is a hollow activity. If the planning activities are to have meaning, plans must be translated into action. Action- and results-oriented student affairs professionals understand the importance of implementing strategies to achieve their goals.

Risk-Taking

The willingness and ability of staff members to take action can be influenced positively or negatively by the view others in the organization take toward risks and failure. If members do not have permission to make mistakes in their efforts to advance the institution, there will probably be little risk-taking in the organization (Larson and LaFasto, 1989). Responsible leaders will challenge staff to move beyond the limitations of the status quo, use discretion, and take risks. Risk-taking must be strategic and consistent with the level of goals. When the organization's vision is grand and bold, the risk-taking necessary to achieve success will grow relationally (Calvert, 1993). Leaders must walk the fine line between being bold risk-takers and being reckless and irresponsible. Though there will never be absolute certainty in the outcomes of any action that leaders take, decision making must take into account the likelihood of success or failure. Responsible leaders and managers will factor into their decision making potential gains associated with risks, what might be lost, consequences of taking action, and the consequences of not taking action. Most important, risk-takers will gather as much information as possible before taking action. The need for credible sources from whom to gather information reinforces the value of having knowledgeable, competent colleagues. Risk-taking is made safer by reliable information. As a dimension of good practice, student affairs staffs will create a culture where credible information is accessible and shared.

A Sense of Urgency

One of the major obstacles to aligning student affairs professionals to act in support of an institution's most pressing needs is the fear associated with change. Because change represents a departure from what is known, the thought of it causes many people to feel at-risk or uncomfortable. Leaders often respond to displays of discomfort or the complaints from those who fear change and work for "compromise" solutions to issues around which compromise will be insufficient in bringing the needed results. In challenging times, leaders must cultivate healthy discomfort. They must do everything possible to develop a sense of urgency about creating a high-performing student affairs program. Developing a sense of urgency is not to be confused with creating panic, fear, or other immobilizing feelings.

Creating a sense of urgency establishes an environment in which the human and fiscal resources can be focused on the areas of greatest institutional need. During times of complacency, resources tend to be focused on areas of interest or comfort. Creating a sense of urgency necessitates the kind of boldness and risk-taking associated with good leadership (Kotter, 1996).

According to Kotter (1996) complacency is nurtured in organizations by issues such as the absence of a major and visible crisis, low overall performance standards, and lack of sufficient performance feedback from external sources (p. 40). If we compare these conditions of complacency with the situations under which many student affairs divisions are functioning, complacency would not seem to be a problem. Energies should be directed at ensuring soundness in the construction of student affairs cultures, programs, relationships, priorities, and activities.

Competence and Learning

The need for competent and knowledgeable student affairs educators is essential if organizations hope to be successful. The skills and knowledge people possess must be compatible with the roles, functions, and responsibilities they will have at the institution. In most cases, people do not come to the campus possessing all the attributes they need to achieve high-level effectiveness; there must be mechanisms in place to help them develop in relation to their job responsibilities (Roper, 1996; Stimpson, 1993).

In a changing society, knowledge and skills can soon become outdated if learning experiences are not available for staff members. In recent years much has been written about "learning organizations" (Schein, 1992; Senge, 1990a). According to Senge (1990a) a learning organization is one "that is continually expanding its capacity to create its future" (p. 14). Such organizations possess the ability to learn in ways that enhance their survival, but more important, through "generative learning" they constantly broaden their creative potential. Such environments encourage and support career-long learners while enhancing their ability to act with care toward the institution and its resources.

Professionals must allocate and manage funds in the most responsible and mission-supportive way possible. When student affairs programs are directed by a vision, the vision can be used to recruit staff capable of achieving the desired objectives (Larson and LaFasto, 1989). By hiring, retaining, and educating effective professionals, the potential of the contributions of student affairs programs is enhanced.

Commitment to Growth

The most responsible actions that student affairs professionals can exhibit are behaviors that show that their primary concern is for the growth of their institution and its members. Learning activities initiated, messages communicated, energy expended, resources allocated, and standards reinforced are among the many ways one can evaluate the importance that student affairs staff give to promoting individual and institutional growth.

Though some institutions find themselves in situations where they are attempting to guarantee survival, few have mere survival as their ultimate goal. Institutional aspirations are more lofty than simply coping with current conditions. Effective leadership and planning, combined with competent staff and appropriately targeted resources, offer a context for promoting institutional growth. Organizations that focus on promoting growth in themselves and their members will, in Senge's (1990a) words, create "paths of development" for themselves (p. 8).

Student affairs staff can be the architects that pave the paths leading institutions to develop. They can do this through joint planning with academic affairs and institutional colleagues, focusing on developing skills among staff, committing to innovation in practice, thinking broadly about student affairs work and how it can best serve the institution, and staying firmly linked to the expressed mission of the institution. At the heart of promoting institutional and personal growth are acting responsibly and acting with concern in the colleges and universities we serve.

Dimensions of Responsible Stewardship

Leadership has been defined by Hersey and Blanchard (1982) as the attempt to influence the behavior of an individual or group, regardless of whether the leader's purpose is based on personal goals, professional standards, or organizational priorities. They define management more narrowly as a special kind of leadership used to work with and through individuals and groups to accomplish organizational goals (p. 3).

As we have emphasized in this chapter, student affairs professionals must be leaders who understand the mission, context, and culture of their particular institutions. They must be skilled at developing initiatives and conveying a sense of vision while being realistic about obstacles and limits, and be creative in mobilizing human and financial resources in a highly focused way. Within and beyond the institution's mission, they must also be true to the mission of student affairs, which has as its overarching goal the promotion of student learning in the most holistic sense of the word.

Theory and research about student development, learning and cognition, communication, leadership, and program design and implementation give us maps for navigating and lenses for seeing more clearly. Principles of good practice provide compasses that help us move in the right direction. But no matter how well grounded we are in theory and research, we need core competencies and qualities to effectively deliver services and achieve institutional goals. One way to conceptualize these core competencies is to place them in four domains: individual competencies and characteristics, interpersonal skills, small group/team-building skills, and organizational skills.

Student affairs professionals need to balance technical and conceptual skill. To be responsible managers, we must become adept at the specialized technical skills needed for our particular role and expand our use of the technologies available, especially the computer hardware and software that are revolutionizing the workplace. Our conceptual knowledge should rest on a solid foundation of knowledge about student demographics and characteristics, student development theory and research, and student affairs values and principles. It also includes knowledge of policies, procedures, people, and systems in our home institution. This knowledge needs to be constantly updated.

There are additional qualities that each individual brings to his or her leadership role. Young (1996), in describing the evolution of the profession's values, noted that the character of the student affairs dean was important, since he or she should be an exemplary individual. The ideal dean "was a generalist, an educator, a symbol of the finest human virtues, a personality, a role model, an inspirer, a guide, a philosopher, and a friend" (p. 89). Although this requirement may seem quaint, there are personal attributes that student affairs leaders have been advised to cultivate. For example, Sandeen (1991) proposed that effective student affairs managers establish trust by demonstrating genuine concern for others, honesty, hard work, and strong commitments to ethical practices. They should "learn to take the heat," insist on excellence, and show compassion and sensitivity for others.

Other individual qualities include a high level of self-awareness (particularly of our own strengths and biases), willingness to ask for feedback, the wisdom to engage others to complement our strengths and help us learn, a sense of purpose, the ability to maintain credibility by acting with intentionality and integrity, objectivity, self-discipline, thoughtfulness, attention to detail, courage, patience, humor, astuteness, and the ability to renew one's energy and enjoy the work.

Interpersonal Competencies

Hersey and Blanchard (1982) state that though less technical skill is needed as one advances to higher levels in the organization, more conceptual skill is necessary (p. 8). The common denominator at all levels of management is human relations skill—ability and judgment in working with and through people. At the heart of this domain is a caring ability to appreciate each individual. It is relatively easy to sense the energy of a working unit. It can be charged with tension or buoyed by informality and enjoyment. Employees have an emotional bottom line about whether they feel supported and validated by their supervisors or whether they feel pressured, overlooked, and demoralized. The leader sets the tone and, as with students, must strike the balance between high expectations and sensitive support.

Whatever the particular chemistry of personalities on the staff, interpersonal effectiveness is increased by the conscious use of communication skills. This entails choosing from a range of skills as a surgeon would choose just the right instrument for a particular purpose. Ivey's (1988) microskills model for interviewing and counseling conceptualizes a hierarchy of communication skills. At the base are attending skills designed for receiving accurately what others are saying; at the top are influencing skills aimed at sending specific kinds of messages. Since managers spend a great deal of time listening, they need to be experts at paying attention, encouraging, observing, asking clarifying questions, paraphrasing, summarizing, and concisely reflecting what the speaker is feeling or assuming. Moving up the hierarchy, managers influence the flow of communication by offering information or suggestions, sharing opinions or self-disclosing, giving feedback, examining consequences, and (most influential), giving directives or confronting discrepancies.

Small Group/Team-Building Competencies

Skilled facilitators with good process skills are vital for team building. Whether we are conducting a meeting or participating in it, student affairs staff members need to use skills that will help the group complete its task and maintain effective relationships among its members.

Skilled communicators and process facilitators are needed in every formal and informal interaction and are especially important when there are morale or performance problems. Whatever style is used, the overall goal should be a highly effective team. Though external evaluators may rate the division in terms of resources and service delivery, managers in student affairs may want to do their own research on how well the team is functioning.

Organizational Competencies

High levels of individual, interpersonal, and team effectiveness help the overall organization. A student affairs division is an organization within the larger whole. It is perceived as effective if it is responsibly meeting goals valued by institutional leaders, which ideally includes contributing to student development, and maintaining positive working relationships. What determines organizational effectiveness? In addition to visionary leadership and competent management, the student affairs division needs sufficient resources, support from the president and other key administrators, effective policies and procedures for rational decision making, and high motivation and morale.

Some of these variables are beyond the control of student affairs leaders. However, in addition to understanding the players and the rules of the game on a particular campus, the student affairs leader needs two important tools for organizational impact: (1) the ability to use different kinds of power, and (2) the ability to orchestrate and adapt to change.

Administrators have formal power conferred by rank—the power to reward or coerce, and the power to control human and financial resources and determine priorities. They can increase our formal power by increasing their ability to provide funds, space, furniture, equipment, or other tangible or intangible goods considered valuable by staff. The flip side is the option to withhold or limit, to gather negative information, or to punish or criticize—an extremely risky strategy, since coercive or punitive tactics almost always breed resentment. They can also increase their legitimate power by changing their role or title (which could also involve getting elected or receiving an award), or changing people's expectations by taking on new duties.

Other kinds of power are not based on formal rank but are earned or conferred. Cuming (1981) describes ways to increase expert, referent, and associative power. *Expert power* is the capacity to influence because of the knowledge or skills a person has or is presumed to have. *Referent power* is based on being liked, admired, and identified with. *Associative power* is based on who one knows. Expert power can be increased through competent performance, visibility, and accomplishment of tasks that have relevance to the powers that be. Referent power can be increased by building trust, identifying common interests, making positive things happen, fulfilling formal and informal contracts, using shared language, and strengthening alliances. Associative power can be increased by getting to know important people, networking with intermediaries, and circulating outside our familiar niche.

Cuming (1981) also describes four influence strategies related to formal and informal power: involvement, enlistment, negotiation, and direction. Involvement and enlistment rely on the power of expertise and relationships. Negotiation and direction rely on the power of position. The involvement strategy invites others to share ideas and design solutions, without preconceived expectations of what they will come up with. The enlistment strategy asks for support for specific proposals. Negotiation involves bargaining and compromising. Directing involves giving instructions without options, with implied or explicit consequences for noncompliance. The leader's skilled use of power has a major impact on productivity and morale.

Power and conscious communication are of great importance when the change is being initiated. Hersey and Blanchard (1982) delineate four levels of change: (1) changes in knowledge are the easiest to make, since they can occur as a result of reading, hearing a new idea from a respected person, or other learning experience; (2) changes in attitude are more difficult because of the positive or negative emotion invested in a point of view; (3) changes in individual behavior are significantly more difficult and time-consuming; (4) changes within groups or organizations are the most difficult to implement, especially if it affects customs, norms, and traditions established over many years.

Ideally, evolutionary change occurs when the group gets new information, or sees a discrepancy between current practices and preferred possibilities, and then works on a plan to close the gap. A single "lone ranger" innovator or perhaps a small group who have gone to a conference together often lead this change. Their eagerness to experiment may attract some early adopters. If the initial steps look promising, the majority may buy in but may demand evidence that the change is really warranted. And there will always be some entrenched resistors.

Disruptive change may be imposed by some external force, political decision, or what Satir called "a foreign element" (Wahbe, 1990). Satir observed that when the status quo is disrupted, even if it is a relatively positive change, a period of "chaos" ensues, during which there is much discomfort and upheaval and often a wish to return to the old reality. The chaos, she proposed, is a necessary part of any growth process for an individual, family, organization, or nation. It requires moving out of the comfort zone and adapting to the demands of the environment and/or practicing new ways of thinking and acting. With support (internal and external) and practice, movement toward integration and a more complex level of stability occurs. Lewin (1947) first identified a similar three-stage process: unfreezing, changing, and refreezing. The unfreezing process creates a readiness for change, and it may be helped by being removed from accustomed routines and relationships. Change then occurs through identification with new models and/or internalization (new behaviors are demanded). Refreezing involves the integration of the new, with reinforcement.

Whether the change is welcomed or resented, effective leaders must help the process move forward by minimizing the anxiety, anger, and inevitable circling of wagons. This may mean increasing the opportunity for discussion and clarification, expecting a certain amount of venting. Questions are answered, expectations are clarified, and productivity and confidence return. Ground rules or guiding principles, plus careful facilitation skills, can help focus the debates and channel the energy.

Skills for Responsible Stewardship

Student affairs divisions are fortunate when they include professionals who have completed graduate programs in student affairs administration or higher education. But some practitioners do not have this background. Furthermore, some graduate programs do not include course work in management and leadership. If they do, they may use textbooks or materials that are difficult to apply in the higher education setting. To be ready for administration, professionals need more than the traditional foundation courses on the history and values of student affairs, student development theories, research methods, and current issues. They need practical skills for responsible stewardship, such as those delineated by Barr and Associates (1993): program planning, program evaluation, outcomes assessment, budgeting and fiscal management, translating theory into practice, understanding legal constraints on practice, developing effective campus and community relationships, conflict management skills, maintaining high ethical standards, and dealing with campus crises. Student affairs professionals need additional skills, which include personnel management, organizing and prioritizing, delegating, monitoring and reporting, and fostering professional development.

Without credibility as effective managers, student affairs leaders may have great theories but no support for applying them. Building and using these skills enable student affairs leaders to implement the fifth principle of good practice: using resources effectively to achieve institutional missions and goals, being responsible stewards of their institutions' financial and human resources, and using principles of organizational planning to create and improve learning environments. To have the greatest positive effect on student development, student affairs leaders need to continue moving in the direction, identified by Sandeen (1991), from a peripheral or adjunct service into the main educational arena of the campus. The chief student affairs officer "is now part of the central management team of the institution and has assumed responsibilities it did not include years ago, and this 'news' ought to be made known to others in and out of higher education" (p. 9). Sandeen fears that faculty, academic deans, business officers, and governing boards may hold stereotypic or distorted ideas about the role of student affairs leaders, and therefore the leaders need to be vocal and visible in expertly carrying out management functions and in leading their divisions' contributions to institutional goals and student learning. In this way, they can meet the dual challenge of being effective, responsible managers as well as inspired, visionary leaders.

7

Forging Educational Partnerships That Advance Student Learning

Charles C. Schroeder

Good practice in student affairs develops structures that support collaboration. Partners for learning include students, faculty, academic administrators, staff, and others inside and outside the institution. Collaboration involves all aspects of the community in the development and implementation of institutional goals and reminds participants of their common commitment to students and their learning. Relationships forged across departments and divisions demonstrate a healthy institutional approach to learning by fostering inclusiveness, bringing multiple perspectives to bear on problems, and affirming shared educational values [ACPA and NASPA, 1997, p. 5].

Higher education continues to be under attack for underperforming its undergraduate education function. As pressures grow for improvement in undergraduate education, colleges and universities are being challenged to become more student-centered as opposed to faculty- or research-centered. Increasingly, they are expected to create learning communities marked by higher levels of student learning and educational attainment. To accomplish these objectives, "Student affairs professionals attempt to make seamless what are often perceived by students to be disjointed, unconnected experiences by bridging organizational boundaries and forging collaborative partnerships with faculty and others to enhance student learning" (American College Personnel Association [ACPA], 1994, p. 3).

This chapter explores the importance of forging educational partnerships that advance student learning, foster educational attainment, and reinvigorate undergraduate education. The first section builds the case for collaboration by illustrating why it is important to create seamless learning environments for students. The obstacles and constraints to collaboration are then reviewed, followed by discussion of various approaches for identifying institutional issues and opportunities that lend themselves to a collaborative response. The next section highlights successful educational partnerships that advance student learning in a variety of campus settings. The chapter concludes with recommendations for building effective educational partnerships.

The Importance of Creating Seamless Learning Environments

Two recent reports on the status of higher education—*An American Imperative: Higher Expectations for Higher Education* (Wingspread Group on Higher Education, 1993a) and *Returning to Our Roots: The Student Experience* (National Association of State Universities and Land-Grant Colleges [NASULGC], 1997)—call for reform of undergraduate education. The reports question the rapid rise in college costs, poor retention and graduation rates, reduced faculty teaching loads, an emphasis on research over teaching, diminished student learning, and lack of service and institutional assistance to local communities and states.

Should reform of undergraduate education be a priority for student affairs educators, or is this a responsibility of academic administrators and the faculty? Addressing this issue is not an option for student affairs but an obligation. So where does student affairs start? Perhaps, with the challenges posed by Terenzini and Pascarella (1994):

> Organizationally and operationally, we have lost sight of the forest. If undergraduate education is to be enhanced,

faculty members, joined by academic and student affairs administrators, must devise ways to deliver undergraduate education that are as comprehensive and integrated as the ways that students actually learn. A whole new mind-set is needed to capitalize on the inter-relatedness of the in- and out-of-class influences on student learning and the functional interconnectedness of academic and student affairs divisions. [p.32]

To address these challenges, student affairs educators must foster collaboration and cross-functional dialogue with faculty colleagues to create a shared vision of a seamless learning environment—an environment where in-class and out-of-class experiences are mutually supporting, where students devote more time and energy to educationally purposeful activities, where institutional resources are marshaled and channeled to achieve complementary learning outcomes, and where students take full advantage of *all* institutional resources for learning (Kuh 1996a, 1997a). A learning environment such as this binds together in a whole and continuous fashion what was once believed to be separate and distinct (for example, in-class and out-of class, curricular and cocurricular) to achieve the "seamless coat of learning" proposed long ago by Whitehead (1929). A seamless learning environment represents a *system* that, according to Deming (1993), is a network of interdependent components that work together to accomplish the aim of the system. Contrast this with the current reality that many students experience. Students' academic experiences are subdivided into a variety of discrete, often disjointed, general education courses and courses in the major. Cocurricular experiences are disconnected from academic experiences. Residence halls are geographically separated from classroom facilities. Campus employment opportunities have no relationship to academic or cocurricular goals, and academic advising and career planning are like two ships passing in the night. Where do students, faculty, and student affairs educators find the connections, the "inter-relatedness" and "functional interconnectedness," the "seamless coat of learning" described by Terenzini, Pascarella, and Whitehead?

The creation of seamless learning environments requires high levels of collaboration so that organizational arrangements and processes can be linked and aligned appropriately (Bloland, Stamatakos, and Rogers, 1996; Garvin, 1993). Although collaboration has been an espoused value for student affairs educators for decades, a variety of obstacles and constraints have made forging effective educational partnerships between academic affairs and student affairs illusive and difficult to achieve.

Obstacles and Constraints to Collaboration

Colleges and universities are unique and distinctive organizations characterized by diverse purposes, organizational structures, and missions. Their strengths can also be their weaknesses and limitations. According to Weick (1983), "Universities are highly differentiated and low on integration, with the basic organizational element (faculty) loosely coupled. The high need for independence and accuracy is basically inconsistent and contradictory with organizational needs of common purpose, common reference, and smooth functioning" (p. 24). Because a primary goal of universities is to create knowledge, faculty must be free to explore and discover the unknown, to break out of current modes of thinking, and to challenge long-held assumptions. Independence, creativity, skepticism, and innovation must not only be encouraged but rewarded if new knowledge is to be created. Developing seamless environments, however, requires creating a shared vision that fosters collaboration and cross-functional dialogue (Kuh, 1996a).

Over the past fifty years, the number of colleges and universities in America has expanded at an exponential rate. In response to burgeoning enrollments, increased governmental intrusiveness, rapid expansion of knowledge, proliferation of disciplines, and diverse student populations, institutions have attempted to address this increased complexity through creating highly specialized hierarchical organizations. Specialization, in turn, has led to increased com-partmentalization and fragmentation, often resulting in what has popularly been described as "functional silos" or "mine shafts." These vertical structures, while often effective at promoting inter-action *within* functional units, create obstacles to interaction, coor-dination, and collaboration *between* units. According to Bonser (1992), "Not only are there barriers between disciplines, depart-ments, and schools, too often warring factions exist within the units themselves" (p. 511). Developing a sense of shared vision and col-lective responsibility for that vision is very difficult when fragmen-tation and compartmentalization foster insular and self-referencing orientations. Faculty, in particular, may view their department as the last bulwark against a hostile and confusing environment in which outsiders (student affairs administrators, politicians, trustees, for example) may make unreasonable demands and even threaten academic freedom (Lovett, 1994).

Tightly coupled bureaucratic organizations, with their emphasis on control and stability rather than on innovation, encourage a sense of predictability, which in turn provides a sense of dominance, security, and control—conditions essential for organizational iden-tity and esteem (Schroeder, Nicholls, and Kuh, 1983). Many divi-sions and departments strive for stability and predictability by creating systems to maintain balance and continuity. There is often great reluctance to changing established practices that may have worked well, regardless of whether they currently work well. Familiar phrases such as, "We've never done it that way before" and "We tried it, but it didn't work" are common. Forging effective col-laborative partnerships to advance student learning requires over-coming this tyranny of custom. Seymour (1995) alludes to the tyranny of the routine and conventional practices when he states, "Most organizations have shared assumptions that protect the status quo and provide few opportunities for learning. Standard operating procedures can become so institutionalized that compe-tence becomes associated with how well one adheres to the rules" (p. 101).

The debilitating effect of the tyranny of custom is best illustrated by the following situation that occurred on a campus where I served as vice president. Shortly after my arrival, I received complaints about the loan disbursement process in my financial aid office. Countless students complained that it took a minimum of two months before they received their financial aid checks. As a consequence, the majority of applicants had to take emergency loans to pay their college expenses. In addition, the cash flow of the institution was negatively affected, and limited funds were available for investment purposes. In exploring this concern, I learned that the financial aid staff blamed the cashier's office for the problem, whereas staff in that office blamed personnel in the university system office, who, in turn, were convinced that the problem was caused by staff in the financial aid office. This cycle of blame had existed for almost twenty years and no one in the three offices—financial aid, cashiers, or the system office—had ever attempted to work collaboratively across boundaries to solve the problem. Why? Because each office staff was focusing on their narrow sets of responsibilities and disregarding the interconnected nature of the loan disbursement *process*. Staff had become detached from a core purpose of the institution—effective student service. As a result, compartmentalization, work process fragmentation, and an "it's not my responsibility" mentality evolved. Because these units operated in relative isolation from one another, a broad array of dysfunctions resulted in what Peter Senge (1990a) refers to as learning disabilities. First, staff in these departments focused only on their positions and demonstrated little responsibility for results produced by the system (that is, sixty-seven days to produce a check). Second, because staff primarily used linear thinking, they were unable to consider the multiple and interconnected issues surrounding the problem. Third, individuals were fixated on short-term events—immediately responding to problems, packaging aid, and so forth—and were thereby unable to see how their actions extended beyond the boundaries of their positions. Finally, staff viewed various events from the confines of their organizational pigeonholes, convinced that they were not responsible and that the problem resided elsewhere.

Fortunately, this story had a happy ending. Directors from the three departments agreed to form a cross-functional team and, as a result, reduced a sixty-seven-day loan disbursement process to nineteen days, thereby improving institutional cash flow, eliminating emergency loans by 70 percent, and reducing staff by the equivalent of three full-time positions—a win-win situation for everyone! This story illustrates an important paradox. Tightly bound organizational entities that provide predictability, stability, and security often unintentionally limit innovation, collaboration across boundaries, and organizational effectiveness (Coate, 1990; Cotter, 1996).

Other potential obstacles and constraints to forging partnerships are traditional views of organizational leadership. In "chain-of-command" hierarchical organizations, direction and power flow from top to bottom. Individuals and units have clearly defined responsibilities, and each is held accountable for carrying them out (Schmidt and Finnegan, 1992). The challenging, changing, and dynamic nature of higher education makes this traditional view of leadership ineffective and obsolete. This old model, where the top thinks and the local acts, must give way to integrated thinking and acting at all levels, cooperation and team work, and collaboration and functional integration. This transformation requires a new view of leadership and it requires leaders who are willing to function as designers, collaborators, teachers, and stewards. According to Peter Senge (1990b), "These roles require new skills: the ability to build shared vision, to bring to the surface and challenge prevailing mental models, and to foster more systemic patterns of thinking" (p. 9).

Forging educational partnerships requires assertive, effective leadership. As Senge suggests, a primary role of leaders is to "bring to the surface and challenge prevailing mental models." Clearly, major obstacles to collaboration are fundamental differences in core assumptions and mental models exhibited by various campus constituencies. For example, faculty, student affairs professionals, academic administrators, and students often have widely differing views regarding the relative merits of in-class and out-of class activities. Well-intentioned efforts to promote collaboration are often derailed because of competing assumptions about what constitutes learning and effective undergraduate education (Kuh, 1997a). The primacy of the curriculum and course work (particularly in the major) are highly valued by faculty whereas informal learning that occurs through out-of-class experiences is not. Similarly, faculty expect students to be independent learners and to exhibit appropriate levels of intellectual self-confidence. Student affairs professionals are sometimes viewed by faculty as "coddlers of the weak and the inept" because they sponsor remedial programs for students who, in the eyes of the faculty, should not have been admitted to the institution in the first place. Similarly, students' views of what really matters in undergraduate education are often quite contrary to those of faculty and student affairs administrators (Kuh, Lyons, et al., 1994). Divergent views and assumptions such as these are rooted in different institutional cultures, and these cultural differences must be understood and appreciated if partnerships are to be developed and sustained.

Blake (1979) has suggested some fundamental cultural differences between faculty and student affairs educators in terms of their personality styles, educational preparation, values, and purposes. For example, for decades we have separated the formal curriculum from the informal cocurriculum. As a result, many student affairs staff view teaching and learning to be the primary responsibility of the faculty. From this perspective, the role of student affairs is ancillary, supplementary, or complementary to the academic mission of the institution. Whitt (1996a) suggests that student affairs educators reinforce separations between in-class and out-of-class learning because they are primarily uncomfortable initiating partnerships with academic colleagues for a variety of reasons, including lack of experience communicating across the cultures of the two groups. This "communication gap" results, in part, from basic value differences between faculty and student affairs cultures. Faculty are often iconoclastic thinkers in their own field who value creation and dissemination of knowledge and autonomy, whereas student affairs values holistic student development and collaboration. Faculty prize thinking, reflection, and collegiality (self-governance, flat hierarchy) over doing, whereas student affairs values teamwork (acceptance of structure and differentiated hierarchy) and doing over thinking and reflecting (Love, Jacobs, Poschini, Hardy, and Kuh, 1993). Simply having different values, assumptions, and responsibilities does not mean that student affairs professionals and faculty members cannot work together or that conflict is inevitable. In fact, if properly acknowledged and utilized, these differences can, at times, enrich and strengthen partnerships (Blake, 1996).

Identify Opportunities for Collaboration

In his Pulitzer Prize-winning novel, *Lonesome Dove*, McMurtry (1991) describes the epic adventure of two aging Texas rangers, Woodrow Call and Augustus McCrae, the first ranchers to drive a herd of cattle from Texas to Montana. The most important member of their Hat Creek organization is the African-American scout, Deets. Each day he is the first to rise, saddle his horse, and ride out twenty miles ahead of the herd, surveying the landscape and identifying areas such as watering holes and grasslands that could benefit the herd, as well as obstacles, such as ravines and canyons, that needed to be avoided. When Deets returned to the herd, he shared his observations with McCall and McCrae, who used the information to make *strategic decisions* regarding the most appropriate routes to achieving their goal.

Scouting has parallels in higher education—we call them boundary spanning and environmental assessment. Environmental scanning, like scouting, requires us to leave the comfort, predictability, and security provided by our organizational boundaries and venture into uncharted, unexplored, and untested terrain. As with the cattle drive, it often requires a reasonable degree of risk-taking, exploration, and systematic assessment to determine progress. Boundary spanning and environmental assessment also help us identify important institutional issues and opportunities that lend themselves to a collaborative response. On many campuses, those issues include developing new approaches to achieving general education outcomes, improving retention and graduation rates by focusing on student success, developing learning environments that integrate curricular and cocurricular experiences, responding to institutional and accrediting agency assessment mandates, fostering civic leadership through community service and service learning activities, and enhancing educational attainment for special student populations. Appropriate responses to institutional issues such as these will vary with the mission, purpose, and size of the institution. On some campuses, particularly smaller ones, collaborative interventions could be focused at the *macrolevel* (institutional level). On larger campuses, the importance of these issues often varies by setting (college, school, department, unit, for example); partnerships could be developed to address them at the *microlevel* (Schroeder and Hurst, 1996). Regardless of the setting, organizational boundary spanning and environmental assessment are essential strategies for determining the issues and opportunities, as well as their relative value to key institutional stakeholders. The importance of this strategy is illustrated by the following examples of "scouting" at my own institution.

During my first two months on campus, I met with the deans and undergraduate deans of every school and college and posed the following question: "What can I and my staff do to help you and your faculty be more successful, particularly with regard to undergraduate education?" These academic leaders described some very interesting issues and opportunities that could best be addressed through collaborative, cross-functional efforts. The dean of agriculture, for example, indicated that his students needed certain skills and competencies (for instance, leadership, interpersonal skills) that could best be developed through cocurricular experiences. The dean of engineering expressed a need for better retention and graduation rates for women and minorities, and the dean of arts and sciences enumerated a range of problems, including poor attendance in large lecture classes, inconsistent advising, limited use of technology to enhance teaching and learning, efforts to improve students' writing performance, and an overall need for more integration and coherence among various disciplines, especially for freshman and sophomore students.

These conversations were the catalyst for educational partnerships that responded to the specific issues raised by the deans and advanced our common educational mission. For example, the Office of Student Life developed a partnership with the College of Agriculture to create a multimedia, interactive CD-ROM software program (*Student Involvement Record*) that helps students assess their skills and competencies and identify out-of-class experiences that are designed to strengthen them. The partnership involved other institutional stakeholders, including the Special Projects Group in Campus Computing, the career center, corporate recruiters, alumni, Residential Life, and the Parents' Association, which provided an initial "development grant" of $5,000. Following the creation of the prototype for agriculture, other deans and their faculty were consulted, and customized versions of the *Student Involvement Record* (SIR) were developed to address specific, yet occasionally different, educational outcomes of interest to faculty in their colleges. As a result, the SIR has become a useful advising and educational planning tool for students with different academic interests. To improve retention and graduation rates for women and minorities in the College of Engineering, staff in Residential Life and the associate dean of engineering developed an Engineering Success Center (learning community) for women interested in engineering. Engineering faculty and staff provided technical support for recruiting, computer lab design, and alumni involvement, and residence life staff facilitated the development of the overall program. Research clearly demonstrates that this "learning community" approach has substantially enhanced student success, retention, academic achievement, and graduation rates for women and minority engineering students. To assist the College of Arts and Sciences in addressing its concerns, a number of partnerships were initiated. The vice chancellor for student affairs and the dean of arts and sciences jointly sponsored a retreat on humanizing large lecture classes and the use of active learning techniques. Similarly, the vice chancellor, in collaboration with the provost, jointly appointed an educational planning quality team to improve advising. Enhancing students' writing performance and bringing a degree of integration and coherence among various disciplines were addressed through the development of twelve residential learning communities primarily for students in the College of Arts and Sciences. In addition, another form of learning communities—Freshman Interest Groups (FIGs)—was created through a similar partnership. This program is described in considerable detail in the next section.

The success of the preceding projects was the result of six strategies. First, major issues and opportunities were identified through boundary spanning and environmental assessment processes. Second, opportunities were created for key institutional stakeholders to develop a shared vision of what mattered, of what was important and worth addressing through collaboration. Third, resources (human, fiscal, and in some cases physical) were linked to achieve mutually agreed upon objectives (for instance, improved retention, enhanced academic achievement, more effective student decision making). Fourth, partnerships involved the development of cross-functional teams of faculty, academic administrators, students, and student affairs educators committed to common purposes and educational outcomes. Fifth, senior administrators were strong champions and advocates for innovation and change and made visible commitments to the various initiatives. Finally, everyone was willing to cross the traditional boundaries between academic affairs and student affairs and pool resources to address common institutional objectives, such as improved academic achievement, retention, and educational attainment.

The next section highlights partnerships that used these and other strategies to overcome many of the obstacles and constraints described earlier. The examples illustrate micro- and macrolevel interventions in a variety of campus settings.

Successful Educational Partnerships

Reinvigorating undergraduate education through creating seamless learning environments has been the focal point of recent institutional reform efforts at various colleges and universities. This section describes six highly successful educational partnerships that were designed to create seamless learning environments. The first three examples reflect microlevel cross-functional interventions, and the last three examples highlight campus-wide, macrolevel partnerships. Each of the six partnerships was developed to address institutional issues, including promoting freshman success, transforming student government into a learning organization, fostering civic engagement through service learning, strengthening community to enhance student learning, establishing and articulating institutional expectations, and reinvigorating undergraduate education through values exploration. Although the institutions cited vary in their mission, purpose, size, and composition, the success of their partnerships is the result of utilizing similar systematic, collaborative, and cross-functional boundary spanning and assessment strategies.

Promoting Freshman Success

With the arrival of a new chancellor, the University of Missouri-Columbia established a goal to "recapture the public's trust" by focusing more attention on promoting student success through enhancing undergraduate experiences. To respond to this mandate, the vice chancellor for student affairs facilitated an educational partnership between arts and sciences, Residential Life, the Campus Writing Program, the English department, and the office of the provost to design residential learning communities that would accomplish the following objectives: substantially enhance academic achievement, retention, and educational attainment for freshmen; make the campus "psychologically small" by creating peer reference groups for new students; purposefully integrate curricular and cocurricular experiences through the development of a seamless learning environment; provide a venue for enabling admitted students to register early for their fall classes; and encourage faculty to integrate ideas, concepts, content, writing, assessment, and research from their various disciplines, thereby enhancing general education outcomes for students.

Using elements of programs at the Universities of Oregon and Washington, a cross-functional planning team composed of academic administrators, residential life staff, faculty, and others developed the Freshman Interest Groups (FIGs) program to accomplish the preceding objectives. In the fall 1995, the program consisted of twenty-two learning communities organized around general academic themes (for example, society and science, ancient people and culture, America's diversity) (Minor, 1997). On average, fifteen to twenty students were enrolled in each FIG, and students lived together on the same floor in a residence hall and were coenrolled in three courses during the fall semester. Each FIG also had a peer adviser (that is, a junior or senior with a major related to the FIG theme) who lived with the students in the residence halls and cofacilitated a one-hour weekly proseminar with a faculty or staff member. The unique curricular and cocurricular structure of the program incorporated the institution's general education, writing-across-the-curriculum, service learning, and learning communities initiatives, and has become a model for integrating a complex mix of subject matter and institutional logistics at a large university. Since each FIG involves an English 20 writing course, writing assignments have provided a unifying method for integrated learning; that is, writing assignments serve to integrate the content of the other courses around the overall FIG theme.

The FIGs program had a major impact on freshman student achievement, retention, and learning. FIGs participants exhibited significantly higher grades, retention rates, and gains in general education outcomes. Students in the FIGs also reported significantly higher levels of academic and social integration and institutional commitment than did other students. They also demonstrated higher levels of involvement, faculty-student interaction, and interaction with peers. Perhaps most significant, the academic and intellectual content of these interactions was significantly higher for FIGs students (Pike, 1996).

The initial cost of the program was split in the first year between the vice chancellor for student affairs and the associate dean of the College of Arts and Sciences. Based upon the dramatic, empirically verified results of the initiative, the program was expanded from 285 students in 1995 to 800 students in 1997. The total cost is now funded jointly by the chancellor (50 percent), the provost (25 percent), and the vice chancellor for student affairs (25 percent).

This partnership was effective because of the strong advocacy and leadership on the part of senior administrators; the development of cross-functional teams that provided opportunities for ongoing dialogue, cooperation, and collaborative planning among key stakeholders; an educational vision that addressed specific institutional concerns; a well-developed assessment plan; and a willingness on the part of various stakeholders to examine carefully core assumptions about the nature of learning and the importance of creating seamless learning environments that integrated curricular and co-curricular experiences for freshmen.

Transforming Student Government into a Learning Organization

In an effort to transform his institution, the president of Samford University launched an ambitious Total Quality Management (TQM) and Continuous Quality Improvement (CQI) program (Corts, 1997). A centerpiece of the program was the Student First

Quality Quest, an initiative designed to give students an opportunity to make recommendations about ways to improve university programs and services. The president's emphasis on "students as customers" and his sincere desire to invite students' participation in the transformation process led the president of the Student Government Association (SGA) to consider the value of using quality principles to transform the SGA. By creating cross-functional teams of student leaders, the SGA president developed a twenty-two member core learning team. The team completed a comprehensive TQM and CQI training program and subsequently created a crisp mission statement that represented the first step in transforming the Student Government Association into a learning organization. The mission of the Samford SGA is "To serve, lead, and nurture the Samford University student body through cooperative efforts with faculty members, administrative officials, and community leaders, all the while striving to enhance the learning community, to build community partnerships, and to advance the overall condition of the university community" (Motley and Corts, 1996, p. 29). Guided by the work of Peter Senge (1990a), *The Fifth Discipline,* Ernest Boyer (1987), *College: The Undergraduate Experience in America,* and Lippitt, Langseth, and Mossop (1985), *Implementing Organizational Change,* the core learning team used quality principles such as systemic thinking, cross-functional collaboration, and strategic planning to assist team members envision the preferred future of student government. A major contribution of the SGA core-team was the development of a seventeen-item action agenda that helped the university president accomplish the institution's strategic plan. Hence, the partnerships formed *within* student government led to effective partnerships *between* the SGA and the university administration. The partnerships succeeded primarily because of the unusual collaboration that existed between student leaders and the university administration and the willingness, particularly on the part of the president of SGA, to examine carefully the prevailing assumptions about the nature of student government on a college campus. The insulated, self-serving, parochial role of SGA was replaced with a dynamic, strategic commitment to institutional change and renewal.

Fostering Civic Engagement Through Service Learning

At Georgetown University, a unique educational partnership has been developed between student affairs educators and faculty to foster students' civic engagement through a range of service learning initiatives. The Volunteer and Public Service Center (VPS) in the division of student affairs provides primary educational and administrative leadership for service learning across the campus. A major component of the VPS program is Georgetown's Fourth Credit Hour Option whereby students from a range of disciplines—social science, English, theology, chemistry, math, Italian, and German—engage in forty hours of service to the community for which they earn credit for one more course. Student affairs educators facilitate ongoing reflection sessions required of Fourth Credit Hour Option students. These sessions help students consider the pedagogical dimensions of service and learning from interdisciplinary perspectives. Staff in the VPS center also partner with faculty to secure additional institutional support for service learning and to design and implement an ongoing, comprehensive faculty development program dedicated to advancing service-learning initiatives across the curriculum. According to the interim director of the VPS Center, the educational partnership developed between students and academic affairs works primarily because, "student affairs professionals envision their role as educators in this partnership. We can teach faculty how to facilitate reflection . . . [and] we contribute powerfully to students' learning by challenging students to connect their service-learning experiences to social problems, policy questions, and ethical dilemmas in ways that further enhance their understanding of the discipline they are studying" (Engstrom and Tinto, 1997, p. 11). Creating the "connections" through systematically integrating curricular and cocurricular experiences is, indeed, a key to the success of educational partnerships, not only at Georgetown but also at other institutions cited in this section. Another, often less obvious, reason for successes of this nature is the recognition and acceptance of the complementarity between student affairs and faculty roles. At Georgetown, faculty assume primary responsibility for defining course goals and clarifying how service learning experiences support the goals and maintain standards of academic integrity and rigor. Student affairs professionals make connections with community agencies, train peer facilitators, and share their knowledge concerning different learning styles and the intellectual development of college students. Clearly, the blend of these different perspectives and skills enriches the overall program and enables it to accomplish its primary objectives—fostering civic engagement on the part of students.

The preceding examples of microlevel partnership intervention had a significant impact on specific campus settings and on the institutions themselves. Partnerships of this nature often create a synergistic effect between microlevel interventions and overall institutional impact. This is further demonstrated by the following examples.

Strengthening Community to Enhance Student Learning

Under the leadership of the vice president for student affairs, the University of Wyoming designed a macroenvironment conference "Building Community for Student Success." Guided by the seven core conditions of an optimal learning environment advanced by Blocher (1978), the six principles of community enumerated by Boyer (1990), and certain elements of the Student Learning Imperative (ACPA, 1994), a cross-functional planning group composed of leaders from academic units, student affairs, finance, administration, and the student association created a seven-hour conference for 100 selected campus, community, and state leaders. The primary purpose of the conference was to develop a set of action strategies and recommendations for enhancing the macrolevel (institutional) learning environment by focusing more on how students learn along with what they learn through connecting, in a more seamless fashion, curricular and cocurricular opportunities. A total of 108 recommendations were included in the final conference report. Most notable among them were ones that emphasized values clarification activities in curricular and cocurricular settings, faculty/staff collaboration in residence halls' theme floors, a scholarly code of conduct for the classroom emphasizing civility and respect, greater staff involvement in the Center for Teaching Excellence activities, a new structure that emphasized collaborative university governance, and an institutional reward structure focusing on collaborative and interunit functioning (Schroeder and Hurst, 1996). The conference represented the first time in the institution's history that representatives from all campus constituencies participated in a program on thematic topics with a common goal.

Establishing and Articulating Institutional Expectations

Concerns about alarming student behaviors, such as academic dishonesty, hazing, date rape, sexual harassment, and other acts of incivility, prompted the vice president for student affairs at the University of South Carolina to examine carefully the nature of the student institutional relationship, particularly with regard to institutional expectations of student conduct and performance. After initiating a culture audit, academic and student affairs staff were shocked to discover that students' behavior was rarely influenced or informed by the institution's culture. Among the most alarming finding was that the university's ethics governing relationships among students and its expectations of student behavior were not clearly articulated (Pruitt, 1996). After discussing these findings with other senior administrators at the institution, the vice president appointed cross-functional teams to identify community values and standards that could be stated more clearly, circulated more effectively, and promoted more intentionally. The result was the development of the Carolinian Creed—a document that captures and articulates the University of South Carolina's standards, expectations, ideals, and aspirations. Because all campus constituents were represented in the development of the creed, the document is widely used to articulate institutional expectations in classrooms, residence halls, Greek organizations, and faculty meetings. A variety of institutional assessments suggest that the creed has had a major impact on improving peer relationships and civility by making *explicit* expectations associated with membership in an academic community.

Reinvigorating Undergraduate Education Through Values Exploration

Like many institutions, LeMoyne College had become increasingly concerned about students' inability to make connections between their courses and their life outside the classroom. As a Jesuit, Catholic institution committed to the "formation of men and women for others," faculty and staff struggled to integrate a traditional liberal arts emphasis with a commitment to social responsibility. In response to a values audit that revealed significant gaps between the assertions and the realities of the institution, a cross-functional team, the Working Group on Values, was created to bridge the gap. The resulting Values Program is designed to engage the college community in a campus-wide education effort to discover and implement ways to help students heighten their awareness of values issues, develop a comprehensive framework for addressing these issues, and strengthen their moral courage to act on their principles (Kirby, 1991). Four major components—the Summer Institute, the Academic Forum, assessment and research, and dissemination and outreach—compose the overall program. The most distinctive feature of the program is cross-functional communication and collaboration among disciplines and programs to design values-based learning experiences for students. These usually reflect a commitment to a year-long theme, such as "Discovering the Sacred in Our Midst: Spiritual Dimensions of Higher

Education," or a weekly theme, such as "South Africa-LeMoyne," a student-generated event designed to focus campus attention on the debilitating affects of apartheid. The Academic Forum provides opportunities for faculty, staff, and students to create events around values themes, all of which emphasize values exploration as opposed to indoctrination. By forging educational partnerships that bring all campus constituents together around a fundamental core principle—values—LeMoyne College has undergone a significant institutional transformation by bridging the gap between espoused values and values in practice.

Building Effective Educational Partnerships

As evidenced by the preceding examples, educational partnerships do not occur serendipitously. They are the result of careful planning, development, and nurturing. Effective partnerships reflect a variety of human qualities—openness, commitment, honesty, trust, mutual respect, and a willingness to compromise. They also require a long-term perspective—after all, Rome wasn't built in a day.

The following recommendations can serve as useful guidelines to develop, nurture, and sustain educational partnerships that advance student learning:

1. Use boundary spanning and environmental assessment to identify institutional issues, themes, problems, and opportunities that lend themselves to a collaborative response. Issues such as improving retention, graduation rates, academic achievement, student learning, and general education outcomes represent overlap areas between academic affairs and student affairs and therefore can provide the common framework within which collaborative partnerships can be created.

2. Develop effective relationships with key institutional constituents, particularly academic administrators (deans, undergraduate deans, department heads and program chairs), faculty, and student leaders. Sponsor a retreat or seminar for these constituents

that focuses on building collaborative partnerships to enhance undergraduate education. Arrange frequent meetings, formal and informal, between student affairs and academic administrators to discuss how residence halls, student activities, and other student affairs units can become locales for student learning.

3. Forge alliances with colleagues in faculty development programs, academic advising, the learning center, and academic enrichment programs—functional units that straddle academic and student affairs. Staff from these areas generally understand the unique differences between student affairs and faculty cultures and are often best positioned to create linkages and connections between these areas.

4. Build partnerships around a shared vision of what matters in undergraduate education and establish clear program purposes with measurable educational outcomes. Use a variety of assessment methods, qualitative and quantitative, to measure the effectiveness of various partnerships. Systematically communicate successes throughout the institution, thereby garnering more support for inter-unit collaboration.

5. Create cross-functional teams composed of people representing diverse characteristics and different functional areas. Creative and innovative responses to institutional problems require the blending of diverse perspectives, and linking and aligning resources from different institutional units. This requires understanding, accepting, and respecting the diverse perspectives and values shared by faculty, student affairs educators, students, and others.

6. Publicly recognize and honor faculty and academic administrators who engage in collaborative partnerships that enhance student learning in and outside the classroom. In addition, provide small stipends for faculty who serve as consultants and affiliates to student affairs units.

7. Utilize space—in the unions, residence halls, and Greek houses, for instance—to support structured learning activities such as supplemental instruction, subject mastery workshops, study

groups, tutoring, and other educational functions that encourage meaningful interaction between faculty and students.

8. Think and act systemically. Understand the differences between organizational functions and processes. Collaborative partnerships require creating and integrating systems in new ways by crossing organizational and disciplinary boundaries to connect, link, and align people, resources, and concepts to produce mutually valued learning outcomes. After all, partnerships reflect a functional integration as opposed to a functional silo mentality.

9. Implement systematic and ongoing assessment programs for identifying major institutional issues, concerns, and themes that lend themselves to collaboration between academic affairs and student affairs.

10. Finally, be willing to leave the comfort, predictability, and security of organizational boundaries and take some reasonable risks. Overcome the tyranny of custom by constantly challenging prevailing assumptions and traditional, bureaucratic modes of functioning. Remember the old adage: It's easier to apologize than to get permission.

Conclusion

Higher education is in the midst of dramatic and profound change. Reform of undergraduate education is a priority for most colleges and universities. Improving student learning productivity, increasing success rates, developing civic leadership, enhancing multicultural understanding, and achieving higher levels of educational attainment necessitate greater integration between curricular and cocurricular experiences. Addressing these imperatives requires the development of seamless learning environments through forging collaborative partnerships between academic affairs and student affairs. As suggested by the Kellogg Commission (NASULGC, 1997), new forms of educational and administrative leadership are needed because, "Our challenges are no longer technical issues of how to allocate rising revenues, but difficult adaptive problems of how to lead when conditions are constantly changing, resources are tight, expectations are high, and options are limited. We live in an age of transformational, not technical, change. Our leadership, like our institutions, must become transformational as well" (p. v). We can view these challenges as overwhelming threats or as opportunities to develop collaborative partnerships for transforming undergraduate education on our campuses. Such an effort is surely worth our time and attention, so . . . *Carpe diem!*

8

Creating Inclusive Communities

Johnetta Cross Brazzell and Linda Reisser

Student learning occurs best in communities that value diversity, promote social responsibility, encourage discussion and debate, recognize accomplishments, and foster a sense of belonging among their members. Good student affairs practice cultivates supportive environments by encouraging connections among students, faculty, and student affairs practitioners. This interweaving of students' academic, interpersonal, and developmental experiences is a critical institutional role for student affairs [ACPA and NASPA, 1997, p. 5].

This chapter describes essential elements of supportive, inclusive communities, and offers examples of programs and practices that build such communities. We also examine research on the impact of community on learning, and provide recommendations for further research on this topic.

The Evolution of Community as a Student Affairs Value

Student affairs deans evolved in the late nineteenth century in the United States as ad hoc community developers, enforcing conduct codes, organizing and advising extracurricular activities, and presiding over residence halls. As faculty focused their efforts on academic pursuits, student affairs professionals recognized the value of experiences that increased students' intellectual, emotional, social, and ethical development.

Young (1996) described the emergence of core values during the profession's first fifty years. For example, the 1949 version of the student affairs point of view reiterated the central concern of student affairs work: "the development of whole persons interacting in social situations. . . . This assertion implies the two central values of early student affairs work—individuation and community" (Young, 1996, p. 88). That is, student affairs professionals have, from the beginning, valued respect for individual uniqueness, identity, dignity, and wholeness and have believed that students should be responsible participants in the learning process. But student affairs also has always embraced the notion "that an institution of higher education must be a place where people grow by means of meaningful relationships" (Young, 1996, p. 90). Young (1996) and others (Cross, 1996) have found that focusing on both individual and community can create conflicting demands. Indeed, Patricia Cross (1996) noted, "Student affairs professionals tend to see the world of higher education through bifocals, tilting their heads upward one moment to focus on individual students through the bottom portion of their lenses and downward the next to view the broader campus environment through the top portion" (p. 5).

In 1990 the Carnegie Foundation reported on the state of community on U.S. campuses, a state characterized by a decline in the commitment to teaching and learning, a breakdown of civility, and an upsurge of campus crime, racial tensions, and substance abuse. The Carnegie study also provided an eloquent statement of the kind of community that colleges should foster (Carnegie Foundation for the Advancement of Teaching, 1990):

- A purposeful community, where faculty and students share intellectual goals and values

- An open community, where freedom of expression is protected but which has a civility that respects the dignity of all

- A just community with a commitment to heterogeneity and diverse opportunities in the curriculum and social activities, and an honoring of the individual person

- A disciplined community in which the individuals are guided by standards of conduct for academic and social behavior and governance procedures that work for the benefit of all

- A caring community that supports individual well-being through positive relationships, sensitivity, and service to others

- A celebrative community, which unites the campus through rituals that affirm both tradition and change and instill a sense of belonging

This picture of what a campus community can be is appealing. Yet eight years later, the challenges to community building seem as great as ever, as students seem preoccupied with competing for grades, preparing for high-paying jobs, retreating to their computer screens, and sticking with like-minded circles of friends (Levine and Cureton, 1998a). Other forces outside higher education also may profoundly affect shared experience, on and off campus, including the aging of the U.S. population, an increasingly multicultural society, redefinition of individual and social roles (for example, through reduced public funding and fewer social support programs), an increasingly information-based economy, economic restructuring at home and abroad, new definitions of family and home, and a rebirth of social activism (Komives and Woodard; 1996).

An increasingly diverse society will, of course, be reflected in increasingly diverse colleges and universities, where "the need for services for diverse students has been gaining the attention of student affairs professionals for two decades and continues to deserve attention. Campuses have only recently developed strategies to cultivate multicultural awareness in members of the dominant culture. . . . The challenge is to develop a common purpose and a sense of community within the mosaic campus" (Komives and Woodard, 1996, p. 543).

Characteristics of Supportive, Inclusive Communities

What makes a community supportive and inclusive? The brief inventory in Table 8.1 was developed by Reisser (1996) for a presentation on "The Keys to Community" for the 1996 Northwest College Personnel Association conference. It offers some characteristics of strong, supportive communities.

This principle of good practice stipulates inclusiveness as well as support. Every campus should be a lab for fostering openness to other cultures. An inclusive campus community requires staff and students who are comfortable with people from any culture, and whose attitudes, language, and behavior reflect awareness and sensitivity to other cultures and backgrounds. This is an ongoing process, since many barriers still exist, and unconscious insensitivity or offensive remarks can cause recurring divisiveness. Talbot (1996) warned that "not all cultures have been incorporated into higher education. . . . In U.S. society, both historically and to a large degree today, there is a 'dominant, powerful' group or culture that has privileges others do not. Typically and historically, that powerful group has been ascribed the following attributes: white, male, heterosexual, middle- to upper-class, and able-bodied" (p. 382).

Models of multicultural development (Bennett, 1986; Pedersen, 1988; Manning and Coleman-Boatwright, 1991) describe a process of gaining accurate information about existing differences, accepting and revising assumptions about those differences, realizing how much of one's own identity is culturally determined, and learning to interact appropriately with persons from other cultures. Many experts in cross-cultural training believe that individuals (especially

Table 8.1. Inventory of Characteristics of Supportive, Inclusive Communities.

Strong Communities	Weak Communities
Plan ways to welcome, orient, and invite involvement	Provide minimal information; hope newcomers will adapt
Generate a climate of pride, excitement, enjoyment	Tolerate a climate of apathy, disengagement, stress
Offer a variety of activities with good attendance	Offer few activities, or generally have low attendance
Students easily find groups where they can feel comfortable	Students feel alone or marginalized
Diversity is visible	Population looks homogeneous
Individual differences are respected; equality prevails	Inequality, stereotyping, or discrimination exists
Open discussion of controversial issues is valued	There are few forums for debates or differing opinions
Socially responsible behavior is modeled, promoted, and reinforced	Irresponsible actions are overlooked; little emphasis on service or ethics
Accomplishments are publicly honored	Little recognition is provided
A sense of community is explicitly valued and promoted	No intentional strategies are used to reinforce a sense of belonging and pride
Morale and self-esteem are high	Cynicism, hostility, and dissatisfaction recur

whites) should engage in self-exploration and workshops that shed light on racist, sexist, heterosexist systems and the privileges afforded to members of the dominant group (Talbot, 1996). Such privileges include, "but are not limited to, being able to rent an apartment anywhere one can afford it without fear of being turned away for unknown reasons; being able to go shopping without being followed or harassed by the store detective or manager; being able to easily purchase cards, posters, greeting cards, dolls, and other toys featuring people of one's own race; and never being asked to speak for one's entire race. . . . [Of course], this is an uncomfortable thought for most well-meaning individuals who do not see themselves as privileged" (Talbot, 1996, p. 387).

At the core of all models for creating supportive and inclusive communities is the assumption that education extends beyond the formal classroom setting, and that when students become part of the institution, they are joining a community that promises to assist them in building a supportive network that will sustain them not only until they graduate but well beyond. Although not all students enter this learning community with a desire to understand and appreciate others who are different from themselves, good practices, usually spearheaded by student affairs professionals, increase the likelihood this will happen.

The Importance of Building Supportive, Inclusive Communities

Influences on psychosocial and cognitive development during college are the focus of a growing body of research (cf., Astin, 1993; Chickering and Reisser, 1993; Pascarella and Terenzini, 1991; Terenzini, Pascarella, and Blimling, 1996). Among these influences are clearly defined goals and learning outcomes, teaching that encourages active learning and cooperation, and positive student-faculty relationships. Most important, however, are the relationships students develop with other students (Astin, 1993; Terenzini et al., 1996; Whitt, Edison, Pascarella, Nora, and Terenzini, in press).

Student Development

Student subcultures become inclusive and supportive communities when there is diversity of backgrounds and attitudes, and conversations based on differences, shared interests, and mutual support.

Student communities are laboratories for learning. Living and learning environments should be both challenging and supportive, helping students feel welcomed and safe as well as challenging them to examine and respect differences. As Parker Palmer (1987) noted, "Community must become a central concept in ways we teach and learn" (p. 25), as it "incorporates all the essential features associated with effective learning environments—a compelling and unifying purpose, traditions and symbols of membership and participation, and mutual support among institutional members" (Strange, 1996, p. 263).

Student Retention and Success

The connection between a sense of belonging and student success and retention also is clear. Tinto (1993) theorized that persistence to graduation and departure are directly influenced by institutional commitment (motivation to graduate from a specific institution) and goal commitment (motivation to earn a college degree). He proposed that institutional and goal commitments are directly influenced by academic and social integration, or the extent to which an individual identifies with, or shares and incorporates the attitudes and values of, his or her instructors and classmates and becomes a member of the college community (Pascarella and Terenzini, 1991).

Numerous studies have demonstrated the positive effects on development and persistence of living in a residence hall (Astin, 1993; Blimling, 1993; Schroeder, 1994; Tinto, 1993). Some researchers have raised questions about the extent to which this kind of integration can occur at community colleges, since they do not have residence halls. However, Napoli and Wortman (in press) found that academic integration and social integration played a significant role in persistence among community college students, and that students at those colleges found ways other than residence to feel part of a community.

Tinto (1993), in highlighting the importance of institutional "fit," focused student affairs practitioners' attention on what they could do to help the transition between membership in past communities and membership in one of many communities on campus. Student affairs staff have applied this model in designing programs, materials, and facilities, including residence halls, student centers, lounges, athletic facilities, and other venues, to enhance educationally purposeful student interaction. Through their programs and publications, they have tried to help students feel part of their campus, identify with its mission, and take pride in its traditions.

Community in a Multicultural Society

The need to foster community and skills for living in a multicultural society also is a critical role for student affairs. Indeed, questions persist about the extent to which college campuses are making sufficient progress in educating all students for life in a diverse society (cf., Boyer Commission, 1998; NASULGC, 1997; Wilson, 1996). There is evidence, for example, that many white undergraduate students are apathetic, or even hostile, about participation in diverse learning communities (Baxter Magolda, 1997; Levine and Cureton, 1998b, 1998c). In a report of their research on undergraduate students in the 1990s, Levine and Cureton (1998c) noted that "tension regarding diversity and difference runs high across college life. . . . Multiculturalism remains the most unresolved issue on campus today" (p. 7). Tensions about difference are exaggerated by the "Balkanization" of campus communities into special interest groups, many of which are based on race, culture, or sexual orientation (Astin, 1993; Levine and Cureton, 1998b, 1998c, 1998d).

King (1994) proposed that in contrast to past emphases on self-reliance, self-motivation, and individual achievement, future citizenship will involve "interdependence and altruism, creating just and caring communities, showing compassion and respect . . . being productive, responsible, honest, and compassionate members of many communities" (p. 414). In making this shift from individualistic to community-oriented goals, the cultural values of students from historically underrepresented groups such as Asian/Pacific Americans, American Indians, and Hispanic Americans, offer new ways to understand community.

The Impact of Technology on Community

One of the most delicate and challenging tasks in higher education is to retain elements of the past that uniquely define and characterize an institution while boldly embracing new ideas and innovative processes. No campus has been untouched by the advances of technology, particularly computers.

Yet too little thought has been given to how the introduction and saturation of our campuses with these innovations will affect the campus culture, climate, standards, and relationships within the community. Does a sense of community exist on the Internet? How do we build inclusive communities when one can do virtually everything from one's room or home? Should supportive networks consist of more than a chat room? How can we help students blend academic, interpersonal, and developmental experiences if they never come to campus?

In its best form, the educational process is committed to the development of the total person. It becomes a seamless process in which the academic and social environment enables students to become self-confident and culturally and spiritually (not necessarily religiously) enriched. This cannot be a complete process without students' developing an understanding of and appreciation for the multicultural communities of the world and a sense of commitment and responsibility for insuring positive change in these communities. The next section offers some examples of programs and services that contribute to supportive, inclusive communities, and strategies for creating such communities on other campuses.

Creating Supportive and Inclusive Communities

Most institutions of higher education have public statements and action plans supportive of increasing diversity and building diverse learning communities. One must not, however, confuse diversity with inclusiveness. Valuing diversity can entail bringing members of various groups to a campus and leaving it at that. Inclusiveness goes much further by ensuring the existence of an interactive process engaging all members of the community. One cannot, however, have inclusiveness without diversity.

Perhaps one of the greatest contributions any institution of higher education can make to its students is an appreciation for inclusiveness. It is an increasingly difficult task, given the public ambivalence and often outright hostility to anything that reflects diversity, difference, affirmative action, or other like-minded endeavors.

Any commitment to promoting inclusiveness sounds hollow, however, if students cannot encounter and learn to appreciate diversity within their immediate environment. A major challenge for student affairs professionals is assisting students in blending the desire to build personal support networks with the need to build relationships with those who are different from themselves. It is relatively easy for most students to create supportive networks of other individuals who look, dress, and think as they do. It is much more difficult to open oneself to the unknown and different, as such openness can challenge long-held beliefs, generational values, and, occasionally, one's sense of entitlement. Examples of how several colleges have helped students learn to recognize, appreciate, and respect differences and develop inclusive attitudes about diversity follow.

A Leadership Training Initiative at a Four-Year College

Building supportive and inclusive communities requires that true partnerships be created within the institution and across organizational structures. This means that everyone must be "on the same page" and speak in concert about the mission of the institution, goals for student learning and for community development, and the means to achieve those goals. The goals should include helping students gain an understanding of the world that is socially responsible. The magic that is possible at any college cannot happen without cooperation, collaboration, and, most important, a shared vision of what the college can and will achieve.

A leadership training initiative at Spelman College demonstrates how institutional goals for student learning and for creating an inclusive community can be actualized. A major tenet of the college's mission is training leaders. Although no one was prepared to argue that this was not happening, there was a general recognition that a formal process to ensure that all Spelman students had the desired leadership experiences was missing. A companion tenet in the Spelman mission is creating leaders who serve. Students are imbued with a sense of social responsibility that obligates them to become agents of social change.

Therefore, during one academic year, the divisions of student affairs, institutional advancement, and academic affairs designed a formal leadership training program that was specific to the needs of the student body. The program was intended to introduce leadership concepts in the freshman orientation course (implemented through the division of academic affairs), coordinate experiential opportunities through student affairs, and connect students to the Corporate Partners program administered by the division of institutional advancement.

Through this formal process, students come to an academic and cognitive understanding of what leadership means. Intellectually, they must examine and deconstruct old notions of what it means to be a leader. They must then understand theoretically and experientially that the actualization of leadership is a group process requiring a connection among all participants. As students work to understand the theoretical and policy genesis of social concerns and ills, they are compelled to work collectively to fashion projects to address some facet of those concerns. By doing so, they become connected to each other as they work together fostering that "sense of belonging" among their peers. They must bring to bear their academic understanding of these issues, grapple with how they are affected personally, learn what the impact is on their campus community, and learn to work with faculty, staff, and peers to develop long- and short-range goals to eradicate the problems. They learn that a leader is not one who acts alone and in isolation. Further, the endeavor requires a consensus of purpose and process among students, faculty, and staff. It ultimately blends students' academic, interpersonal, and developmental experiences in a format that stretches students' vision of the possibilities offered by the education they are receiving. They come to understand that the acquisition of their education is larger and more important than satisfying their own personal needs. They are obligated to become leaders in their communities and leave them better places than they found them.

Student Programs at a Community College

Community colleges have a greater challenge than four-year institutions in building a sense of community, since their students, many of whom are part-time and most of whom are commuters, may not stay on campus long enough to feel connected to a campus community. But community colleges also have the advantage of small classes, faculty focused on teaching rather than research, and students who are in the midst of life transitions and therefore can be especially receptive to supportive programs or new adventures.

How, then, can community colleges create supportive and inclusive communities? Many create minicommunities through student organizations. For example, at the largest of Suffolk County Community College's three campuses, forty-six student clubs provide opportunities to engage with other students. Some are academically oriented, like the Philosophy Club, History Club, or Criminal Justice Club. Some are based on shared interests, like the

Sailing Club, Ski Club, or Scuba Club, and some are affinity groups, like the African-American Student Union, Latin/Hispanic Club, or the Gay, Lesbian, Bisexual Alliance.

The club program exemplifies a conscious attempt to weave students' academic, interpersonal, and developmental experiences together into a coherent tapestry of learning. It aims not only to build leadership and interpersonal skills but to reinforce community-oriented values and connections with faculty outside the classroom.

Staff members emphasize that each student's individual contribution is important to the group and that each club is part of a larger whole. They reinforce this by bringing all the club officers together regularly to report on their club's activities and to invite cosponsorship of community-minded programs, like a blood drive, food bank drive, scholarship fund-raiser, Earth Day program, or AIDS vigil. At the end of the year, family members and faculty are invited to a recognition ceremony. Individual contributions by student leaders, faculty advisers, and loyal members are honored. The sense of shared community is underscored through slides or videotapes of the faces of friends working and playing together.

Training for officers includes working through hypothetical conflicts, learning to think about the interests of all the members, and working together to plan successful events. Student activities staff members stress appreciation for individual differences as they conduct team-building exercises, and reiterate mottoes that reinforce the value of committed groups. (Examples: "Never doubt that a small group of thoughtful, committed citizens can change the world; indeed, it is the only thing that ever has." "There are no victims; only volunteers." "The best city is generosity.")

The student activities staff at Suffolk County Community College also coordinates a freshman orientation program designed to build an inclusive and supportive community. Student orientation leaders develop important and lasting bonds during intensive training. They welcome new students while wearing T-shirts announcing that "We put the community in Suffolk Community College."

In small group sessions, student orientation leaders use the same ice-breaking exercises they experienced in training to help the new students get to know each other. They strongly advise the new students to get involved, join a club, team, or performing arts group, write for the student newspaper, and attend workshops and multicultural programs. During the first two weeks of the semester, the orientation leaders call their advisees to reinforce support and invite involvement.

A weekly Common Hour was instituted to encourage student participation in community events such as Veterans' Week ceremonies, African-American History Month, Women's Week, and an International Festival, all of which provide a visible invitation to students from different backgrounds to feel welcome on campus. Student relationships are also encouraged through trips to New York City for Broadway shows, Amateur Night at the Apollo Theater in Harlem, cultural events, museum visits, and other experiential learning.

Family-oriented events also are organized to create a sense of community for adult students and their families, who are invited to attend free first-run movies, a Saturday Halloween Festival, and special holiday brunches. The Honor Society gives high-achieving students not only public recognition but also a chance to join a group that shares interests and does community service projects. These are the kinds of activities carried out by many community colleges that promote the formation of lasting relationships, positive identification with the college, self-esteem and caring, a sense of belonging, and strong community spirit.

Finally, Suffolk County Community College has an Honors Program that is deliberately creating an "electronic community." Its faculty have developed a network that enables students to have a dialogue with each other, with faculty, and with alumni. The Honors Program web page has a calendar of upcoming events, including concerts, lectures, transfer information sessions, and plans for a trip to visit Adelphi University for a lecture on Greek tragedy and a performance of "Antigone." Rather than precluding interpersonal connections, the computer networking seems to enhance them. Technology can be a tool for community building rather than a barrier to it.

A New Course on "Pluralism and Diversity in America"

Institutions that are large and heterogeneous must be especially creative in fostering a climate of multicultural awareness. A striking example of a community college's commitment to this idea can be found at Rockland Community College, which initiated a mandatory course on "Pluralism and Diversity in America." The course was designed to increase tolerance by studying the dynamics of intolerance, the role of stereotypes, and the impact of demographic changes in the United States.

In launching this experiment, student affairs professionals worked closely with faculty to prepare for the pilot semester, organizing discussion groups and in-depth workshops with guest resource people who were experts on race, culture, class, gender, sexual orientation, and group process. The requirement that all liberal arts students take this course necessitated that forty sections be offered. This led to a large number of faculty and staff volunteering to teach in interdisciplinary teams, and embarking on a journey to increase their own understanding and appreciation of diversity. They created a new textbook and course materials (Wilder, Sherrier, and Berry, 1991), shared strategies for maintaining a climate of openness and respect, and grappled with the difficult issues arising from such a course.

Extensive evaluation at the midpoint and the end of the first semester revealed that students were moved and heartened by the discoveries they made about themselves and each other, and that they appreciated how carefully the instructors engaged them in an interactive process. Few colleges have gone to such lengths to create a learning experience about diversity for all students. Yet most institutions today have statements or action plans supporting diversity.

Lessons from Special Colleges for Special Students

Valuable lessons for learning how to create inclusive and supportive communities, especially encompassing students of color and
women, can be learned from institutions historically created to serve
the needs of those populations, including historically black colleges
and universities, women's colleges, tribally controlled colleges, and
Hispanic-serving institutions. What are the characteristics of these
institutions that underlie the spirit of the seventh principle of good
student affairs practice? Common threads running through these institutions are (1) student-centeredness, (2) the provision of opportunities to participate in a wide range of student activities, (3) an
environment that fosters pride, and (4) positive relationships between students and faculty (Fleming, 1984; Hispanic Association
of Colleges and Universities, 1991; Horowitz, 1984; Roebuck, and
Murty, 1993; Stein, 1992).

Student-Centeredness

Student-centered institutions organize their programs and services
with the students' interests and needs as priorities. It is easier to create a student-centered community when the size of the institution
is relatively small. Institutions serving women and minorities tend
to be small, thus providing many opportunities for students to feel
connected to peers, faculty, and staff. Larger institutions must strive
to create this sense of smallness by developing enclaves where students can feel special and not be overwhelmed by the numbers
around them. The danger of creating such enclaves is a loss of community throughout the institution, the development of cliques
(noninclusiveness), and the possibility of students' falling through
the cracks.

There are other ways to be student-centered, however, besides
creating welcoming niches for students. Student-centeredness is reflected in activities and curricular offerings designed to be relevant
to students' interests and backgrounds, systems and procedures that

provide convenience and flexibility, assessment strategies that clarify where students are when they enter and help them build on their strengths, and staff members who place contact with students above other work activities, to name a few examples.

Opportunities to Participate

The greater the opportunity for students to participate in a range of activities, the more likely they are to feel a part of their community and to become productive contributors. Students who participate in student government, cocurricular clubs and activities, and fraternities and sororities are able, with the assistance of student affairs professionals, to translate new skills and college experiences into career enhancers and to gain a greater understanding of the larger society.

Pride

A major factor guiding the decision of minorities and women to attend institutions that provide a mirror for them is the sense of pride they derive from being in such environments. They are immersed in an educational experience that provides them with positive feedback about their identity, history, and traditions. Positive reinforcement fosters pride. For example, women's studies programs on all-female campuses provide an especially supportive environment for female students to learn about themselves. Historically black colleges and universities explore black consciousness, culture, and history. Tribally controlled colleges emphasize tribal history and culturally specific philosophy.

Student-Faculty Relationships

Students who can cite a meaningful relationship with at least one faculty or staff member during their college years are more apt to have a fulfilling, enriching experience. They are more likely to feel supported and integrated into campus life. Institutions such as women's colleges, community colleges, and those focused on minorities tend to have a strong emphasis on teaching. It is a reflection of the student-centered, hands-on nature of the education provided. In such institutions, teachers serve as role models. Because the size of the campus community tends to be small, there is a greater opportunity for personalized interaction both inside and outside the classroom. Students feel valued, connected, and special. In such settings, faculty and student affairs professionals are more apt to work in partnerships to create a supportive environment. Faculty are more likely to be familiar with the range of support services provided in the student affairs division and to refer students for those services.

Strategies for Creating Supportive and Inclusive Communities

Ideally, a commitment to building supportive and inclusive communities should be part of the institution's mission and strategic planning process. Student affairs leaders need to advocate for the inclusion of student development principles in those mission statements. For example, at Suffolk Community College, the dean of students worked closely with the dean of instruction to rewrite the "Role and Scope Statement" for the college's Ammerman Campus (1995). It now makes explicit commitments relevant to this chapter: to help students "broaden intellectual, cultural, and aesthetic horizons; gain teamwork and leadership skills; gain a global perspective; increase interpersonal communication skills; become more self-directed while recognizing their interdependence with others; and increase understanding and respect for diversity in all its forms."

The challenge is to live by those values. Shared vision and shared goals foster supportive and inclusive community only if its members consciously strive to create them. Just as we ask student leaders to shift out of their comfort zones in order to learn by trial and error, we can ask our administrators to create action plans and experiments that actively cultivate supportive environments. In our own written and spoken communication, we can reiterate principles of good practice as more than just points made in a conference discussion. We can engage staff members and students in reflecting on these values, use them to renew our focus, and report on what we have accomplished.

Another strategy is to become well-informed about current theory and research on community building. For example, Chickering and Reisser (1993) proposed that for optimum development, the community—whether it takes the form of residence hall unit, sorority or fraternity house, student organization, or informal circle of friends—should (1) encourage regular interactions among students and provide a foundation for ongoing relationships, (2) offer opportunities for collaborating and sharing interests, engaging in meaningful activities, and facing common problems together, (3) be small enough so that no one feels superfluous, (4) include people from diverse backgrounds, (5) serve as a reference group, in which there are boundaries that indicate who is "in" and who is "out," and have explicit or implicit norms about what it means to be a "good" member.

Building on this list, student affairs professionals can be intentional about

- Giving students a reason to congregate and interact, especially with others outside their familiar social or ethnic groups

- Reinforcing collaboration and meaningful shared activities

- Making groups small enough to involve everyone

- Training student leaders and teaching interpersonal skills

- Linking subgroups to the larger community

- Encouraging expression of different points of view

- Using symbols, images, mottoes, logos, colors, decals, and mascots to reinforce a shared vision of community

- Making norms, expectations, and ethical standards explicit

- Holding ceremonies and celebrations that recognize academic, athletic, and artistic achievements

- Drawing students into clubs and committees

- Providing appealing spaces for them to interact informally

- Appreciating anyone known to be cordial and friendly to students, from custodians to security guards

- Proposing topics for faculty meetings or workshops that focus on positive relationships: mentoring skills, collaborative learning, faculty-student interaction, campus climate, and so forth

- Holding convocations, receptions, banquets, and special events that mark the collegiate experience as a communal endeavor

- Training staff in multicultural awareness

- Assuring that student programs reflect "the mosaic campus"

- Initiating proactive efforts to reach out to all students and offer caring, support, and involvement

A final strategy is ongoing assessment of the campus community. What subcultures exist? What norms do they reinforce? How do they reinforce or diminish institutionalized influences? Do they encourage friendships to develop? Do they foster intercultural communication? Do they support or block student development? What are the characteristics of communities that value diversity, promote social responsibility, encourage discussion and debate, recognize accomplishments, and foster a sense of belonging among their members? What strategies work best for building such communities? What kinds of communities do students form when left to their own devices?

Conclusion

Student affairs professionals can play a critical role in assuring that campus communities are inclusive and supportive, as well as vibrant and welcoming. In playing an active role as community developers, we can continue our tradition of direct involvement in student development through interactive learning and the power of relationships. We can build inclusive and supportive communities by embodying an appreciation of individual differences and orchestrating workshops, convocations, and organizations designed to encourage discussion and promote social responsibility. Through our leadership training initiatives, residence life programs, advising, counseling, student activities efforts, and multicultural programs, we can reinforce the value of connecting students' academic, interpersonal, and developmental experiences. In helping to create supportive and inclusive communities, we renew our own commitments to higher education's most important ideals.

9

Using Principles to Improve Practice

Gregory S. Blimling and Elizabeth J. Whitt

Student affairs organizations, like the institutions that maintain them, are challenged to demonstrate their accomplishments and, increasingly, to justify the appropriateness of decisions and policies to external constituents. Newspaper accounts of hate speech, sexual assaults, binge drinking and hazing in fraternities, sexual harassment, widespread use of alcohol and other drugs, academic dishonesty, and student riots after sporting events and festivals focus attention on the worst aspects of student life. Of equal interest to the media are allegations of cultures of political correctness and "value-free" approaches to student behavior. These stories, juxtaposed with descriptions of the high cost of college and the struggles families face to pay for their children's education, raise serious questions about the relative costs and benefits of college, as well as the effectiveness and responsibility of college administrators, especially student affairs staff.

At the same time, student affairs faces challenges from within. One could argue that student development has been the dominant paradigm for student affairs for more than twenty years. Application of theories of human development to eighteen- to twenty-two-year-old college students is at the center of this paradigm, and facilitating development of individual students outside the classroom and in the affective rather than cognitive realms was the primary focus of student affairs work. This movement was intended to create an area of specialization for student affairs professionals—as teachers outside the classroom—of equal value to, yet distinct from, that of faculty (Caple, 1996). Some have argued that this has moved student affairs staff away from the core mission of higher education, student learning, and cognitive development (Bloland, Stamatakos, and Rogers, 1994). Others have asserted that the application of theories of student development to student affairs practice was too complicated to be practical, whereas some criticized the lack of empirical evidence of the impact of theories of student development on student outcomes (Bloland et al., 1994).

The Student Learning Imperative (SLI), developed under the auspices of the American College Personnel Association in 1994, offered a fresh perspective on this debate about the purposes and philosophy of student affairs work. The SLI noted the implications of the learning paradigm for student affairs, and challenged us to define our work in terms of student learning by creating learning-oriented student affairs divisions. These are places where achievement of learning outcomes is the goal of student affairs programs and services, collaboration across student affairs and institutional functions is the norm, resources are allocated with learning goals in mind, and what and how much students learn are the criteria by which effectiveness is evaluated. The SLI also defined student learning in the broadest terms, including cognitive competence, intrapersonal competence, interpersonal competence, and practical competence. The SLI calls us to live up to our historic claim that we are educators concerned with the "whole student" (Blimling and Alschuler, 1996).

The SLI did not, however, tell us *how* to do that. If student-learning-oriented student affairs divisions are a desirable goal, *how* can they be created? *Principles of Good Practice for Student Affairs* is a response to those questions. Student-learning-oriented student affairs divisions can be created through good student affairs practice: engaging students in active learning, helping students develop coherent values and ethical standards, setting and communicating high expectations for learning, using systematic inquiry to improve student and institutional performance, using resources effectively to achieve institutional missions and goals, forging educational partnerships that advance student learning, and building supportive and inclusive communities.

In this chapter, we look at the principles of good practice as a whole. Next we identify elements of the principles of good practice that make for successful student affairs programs and offer seventeen strategies to help implement the principles. The chapter concludes with a case study illustrating how the principles can be used to address a common problem among college students—binge drinking.

Strategies Based on the Principles of Good Practice

Throughout this book, we have identified and described the impact of an array of forces of change on student affairs practice and provided principles of good practice as a means to address the demands and challenges those changes present. Each chapter examined the current higher education context through the lens of a specific "good practice," and offered suggestions for implementing that practice in a variety of student affairs settings.

Although we believe it is useful, even necessary, to identify discrete elements of good student affairs practice, we know that doing so risks ignoring the complex relationships among aspects of student affairs work—just as separating academic and student affairs into separate organizational structures disregards the complex ways students learn and grow (Terenzini et al., 1996). What, then, are the common threads that weave the principles into a rich and complex tapestry of practice? We offer the following seventeen strategies derived from *Principles of Good Practice for Student Affairs:*

1. *Employ ongoing assessment of student outcomes.* Student affairs claims an important role in retention, graduation, and student

learning, but it is difficult to support such claims without evidence. One of the great weaknesses in student affairs organizations has been their inability to demonstrate how their efforts influence student learning. Although research on college impact provides ample indications that there are such influences, too few student affairs professionals take the time to examine how—or whether—their programs and practices contribute to student outcomes. Ongoing and accurate assessment of student outcomes reinforces the value of student affairs to the university community and of the knowledge students acquire. Assessment strengthens student affairs' position as an integral agent in creating learning environments for students, and it allows student affairs to examine what it does well and what it does not do well—and modify the latter. Most important, assessment benefits students by enhancing the capacity of student affairs to meet their learning needs.

2. *Communicate institutional values and expectations through policies, decisions, processes, and interactions.* Institutional values and expectations are conveyed through words and deeds—what is said, as well as what is not said, how authority figures (whether students or senior administrators) behave in times of crisis and of celebration. Values common to academic communities through history include integrity, community, a search for truth, respect and civility toward others, and acceptance of differences. If today's students are to be responsible citizens, these values should be part of their curriculum.

3. *Link the classroom with out-of-classroom activities.* Students experience universities as a whole, and they learn best in environments that blur boundaries between in-class and out-of-class experiences. One of the best examples of such environments is living and learning centers where faculty teach, and perhaps live, in a college residence hall. Research on college impact is clear: The most effective learning experiences and environments are those that engage students in educationally purposeful activities with faculty and peers who challenge them to think in new and different ways (Kuh, 1995, 1996a; Pascarella and Terenzini, 1991; Terenzini et al., 1996).

4. *Provide high-quality services and programs that support student learning.* Much has been said about how student affairs can construct programs to promote student learning. What has not been said enough is that these are built on a foundation of effective student services. A student who cannot get financial aid because the financial aid office is not student-oriented might not be able to enroll. Similarly, a student who lives in a residence hall that is poorly maintained is likely to be more concerned with shelter and comfort than with opportunities to engage in learning activities. The question should never be, Should we emphasize student services or student learning? The question should always be, How do we implement both? Nevertheless, high-quality student services are the start of a strong student affairs organization, not the end. More is required of student affairs than simply well-managed, efficient services.

5. *Establish coherent purposes and learning outcomes appropriate to the backgrounds and aspirations of students and consistent with the institution's mission.* Each program in student affairs should be able to articulate the learning outcomes it strives to foster. These outcomes should be consistent with the institution's mission and consistent with the philosophy of the division of student affairs. Student characteristics define an institution. In identifying desired learning outcomes and designing programs and services to achieve them, student affairs administrators should assess the needs and goals of *their* students—not students they wish they had, or think they have, or used to have.

6. *Communicate to students what is expected of them.* If students know what is expected of them, they are likely to try to achieve it. If they do not receive clear messages from faculty or student affairs staff about expectations, they will look elsewhere, probably to other students. Expectations can be communicated directly, such as through written and spoken statements about "what it means to be a student here." Expectations also can be communicated by how the university celebrates and recognizes accomplishments of groups and individuals—and by who is recognized and who is not. Creating an

ethos of learning, in which all are focused on the educational purposes of the institution, provides clear messages to students about
what is expected of them.

7. *Develop in students a sense of belonging, community, pride, and
loyalty to the institution.* Students want to be proud of their college.
The accomplishments of the faculty, national recognition for high-
quality performance, athletic accomplishments, and other forms of
recognition tend to make students feel good about having selected
an institution and encourage them to feel a part of its accomplishments. Homecoming activities, parents' weekend, and pep rallies
are traditional ways to help build loyalty to the institution and link
the student with the institution. But such traditions—if implemented in ways that exclude experiences and interests of people of
color, for example, or older students—also can make students feel
as though they are unwelcome or outsiders. Finding ways to draw
on the heritage of the past while celebrating the diversity of the present can create ties that bind the whole community.

8. *Encourage student involvement.* The more students are involved, the more they gain from college and the more likely they
are to persist to graduation. Therefore, the more ways we can find
to help engage students, the more they will learn. Whether this engagement is through informal contacts with faculty or through for-
malized out-of-classroom activity such as clubs and organizations is
not important; all educationally purposeful activities offer learning
opportunities. Involvement also tends to create support networks.
Students develop friends and associates to whom they can turn for
questions, guidance, and emotional support.

9. *Value diversity, accept differences among students, and work to
overcome prejudice on campus.* One obligation of universities is to develop educated citizens. Learning environments enriched with diverse views and people of varied backgrounds, races, cultures, and
beliefs promote learning. Openness to diversity and challenge are
fostered not only by interactions with diverse student peers and faculty, but also by institutional commitments to racial understanding

and pluralism (Whitt et al., 1998). Student affairs has the opportunity to support groups and programs that celebrate these differences within the institutional community. Programs such as Kwaanza, Martin Luther King Day, Black History Month, Coming Out Day, Hispanic History Month, and similar programs allow individual students to explore their cultural backgrounds, as well as inform others within the institution of the heritage of underrepresented groups on college campuses. These and similar activities contribute to an institutional ethos that accepts and celebrates differences among people and helps to free people of their misconceptions and prejudices. This commitment must also be reflected in institutional policies, such as public statements about the institution's commitment to multiculturalism and policies that would prohibit discriminatory practices such as residence hall room changes on the basis of race, or student clubs or organizations that exclude members of certain ethnic backgrounds or religious beliefs.

10. *Involve students in institutional governance, policies, and decisions.* As members of the university community, students should have a voice in the policies and procedures that guide it. Students provide a unique and informed perspective on the impact of policies or institutional decisions on students. Perhaps more important, student participation in institutional governance teaches students the process of democratic decision making. This process of deliberation requires critical thinking, negotiating, teamwork skills, speaking skills, and interpersonal skills. Universities should include students in as many committees, task forces, and other deliberative bodies as possible. Each provides a learning opportunity for students and an opportunity for members of the university to gain an additional perspective in making decisions important to the whole university community.

11. *Promote civility on campus.* Students have a right to disagree with decisions made by administrators, faculty, and others. They have a right to protest, write articles in disagreement with the institution, and take other steps to make their viewpoint known. They

do not have a right to vandalize university property, be destructive to the institutional processes of deliberation, or prevent others from carrying out their daily work. Slanderous attacks by individuals against others is never acceptable within the university community. Ideas can be challenged and debated heavily, but individuals should not be the subject of attack. To the extent that student affairs has contacts and relationships with student organizations and individuals who may have issues of disagreement with the administration, they can influence how students and student organizations express this disagreement. It is a responsibility of student affairs to engage students who have an issue of concern with the institution and to help them find constructive means of redress. This is the basic responsibility of every member of the university community—civility toward one another. This is how educated citizens communicate, and it is our responsibility as student affairs educators to ensure that students learn how to express themselves in a civil manner.

12. *Create formal and informal opportunities to engage faculty, staff, and students in ways that contribute to the greater good of the institution.* Sometimes in talking about student affairs organizations, it can appear that student affairs organizations are entities unto themselves with their own agenda separate from that of the institution. Nothing could be further from the truth. Student affairs organizations are a reflection of the campus culture and the community. As such, they have an obligation to engage and support the institution in what it is trying to achieve. Opportunities to interact with faculty and other staff to work on a variety of institutional problems help present student affairs as an integral part of the university community—a member of the institution striving to achieve the same learning and community goals as the rest of the institution. These opportunities, whether social or formal, help to promote the contributions of student affairs to the life of the campus and provide opportunities for student affairs educators to communicate their values and their educational role within the institution. These forums also provide student affairs educators with the opportunity to share their concern

and care about students, thus encouraging an ethos of caring for students in the institutional community.

13. *Develop a student-centered focus.* We believe that student affairs organizations must reaffirm their commitment to being student centered and continue to press for institutions to redefine their mission in terms of students and what students learn. This is not only consistent with the historical mission and philosophy of student affairs, it is the recommendation of virtually every higher education report that has been issued within the past ten years. This student-centered approach is in contrast to what appears to be a move toward a more content-centered education brought about by technology and external economic pressures for efficiencies defined by those outside of higher education. Although there is little debate in the student affairs community about whether higher education should be student centered, there is some debate within the community about what that means and how it is to be implemented.

14. *Create flexible networks of resources.* Given a more highly diverse student body and a much wider array of instructional methods and delivery systems, student affairs must be prepared to change, modify, and specialize resource needs for its diverse group of students. Departments in student affairs need to become less specialized and more capable of understanding how other student affairs areas function so that they can aid students in multiple ways. Technology needs to be developed in student affairs in the same way it is developed in other areas of the university community. Not only should the delivery of financial aid applications, admissions applications, and housing and registration be done via the Internet, other forms of support for students should be available through this mechanism as well.

Student affairs organizations also must be willing to link with other programmatic efforts of the university to form flexible networks that support students. One good example of how this can happen is offered by career development programs. For many years these programs functioned as placement offices where students went to be trained on how to interview and meet with recruiters who came to campuses looking for college graduates. Although this traditional method of operating a placement office will probably continue for some time, technology has made it necessary to consider other avenues to help students and employers connect. Computer systems now exist that allow employers to search through databases of students who meet their specified criteria, examine their resumes, and interview them through videoconferencing. Students have a similar option to screen recruiters and to look at job postings by specifying their search criteria, such as job interest, salary, geographic location. Guidance regarding resumes, counseling about interviews, and examples of interviews are routinely placed on the Internet for students to use.

One advantage of this system is that it is accessible twenty-four hours a day, seven days a week. The student who has time to job search between 10:00 P.M. and 2:00 A.M. has that option on the Internet, as does the student who is taking courses overseas or who is part of an internship or coop experience. Such flexible networks of resources need to become the norm if we are to meet the needs of a more diverse student population of the future.

15. *Use a systemic approach.* For many years, student affairs has been concerned with the individual student. In some ways, this has been seen as forms of individual intervention. Given student affairs' historic roots in counseling and psychology, it is natural that the focus of attention would be on the individual student. Most forms of intervention discussed in the student affairs literature have focused on how individual students change or how individual student behavior problems can be addressed. What has been missing from much of the student affairs' literature has been a greater focus on the student as a member of the group and the influence of the community on student behavior. Some early literature in student affairs (for example, Feldman and Newcomb, 1969) addresses the importance of a student's peer group on student behavior, and recent literature (Astin, 1993; Pascarella and Terenzini, 1991) affirms

the importance of the peer environment on student behavior and achievement. However, there has been little focus in student affairs on taking a more community or sociological approach to looking at students as members of groups. The interest of student affairs educators in the psychosocial, moral, and cognitive development of students may have overshadowed the person–environmental interaction theory and its importance in student learning.

Systemic changes focus on how to change the system in use. The type of systems thinking that we are describing is based on developing the ability to consider long-term cause-and-effect relationships that will change the culture of learning on campus. Examples of systemic thinking can be global. For example, traditionally aged college students eighteen to twenty-one operate on a different sleep cycle than most adults. Anyone who has been in a college residence hall can tell you that students often are awake and active at 2:00 A.M. However, they can easily be sound asleep at 11:00 A.M. What if institutions were to change the normal cycle of class offerings from classes starting at 8:00 A.M. to classes starting no earlier than 9:00 A.M.? Chances are good that students would be more alert and more prepared to engage in their academic work. But universities generally function on a schedule most convenient to faculty and administrators rather than to students. An important systemic change to the organizational structure might be to refocus on what students need rather than what has been traditional.

16. *Increase the intellectual content of student affairs activities*. Many student activities are offered with a minimum of intellectual content. Among these are parties, dances, eating contests, carnival games, and many other recreational kinds of activities. Although student affairs organizations offer more intellectual experiences, such as workshops on leadership, few in the academic community see the latter as representing the major effort of student affairs. Student affairs educators can seize opportunities to generalize learning from a variety of out-of-class activities by thinking through what they want students to learn from the experiences they are structuring,

stating these clearly, and by linking with academic programs to form partnerships.

17. *Create an ethic of caring.* Kuh and colleagues (1991a) found that an ethic of caring about students permeated colleges that they described as the most involving colleges. A campus culture where all the employees have an interest in the students' welfare conveys to students an entirely different message than an institution where students' inquiries are treated as an interruption. Developing an ethic of caring is in part a commitment to courtesy and service to students. But more important, it requires that everyone at the institution recognize the institution's mission and are willing to sacrifice their own personal ambitions to help the institution achieve what is most important—student learning.

Principles of Good Practice in Use: A Case Study

The telephone rang early Sunday morning, November 1. The call was from Mary Arnold, the dean of students. She had spent most of the previous night at the hospital with a student who had consumed eleven glasses of "purple Jesus" (a concoction of grape juice and grain alcohol) at an off-campus party attended by more than four hundred Midwest University (MU) students. Three party guests had been taken to the hospital for excessive consumption of alcohol. Two were expected to make a full recovery, but Pete Fox, a nineteen-year-old sophomore, was struggling for his life. Several members of the local press, who had heard about the incident from contacts in the local police department, were at the hospital interviewing Pete's friends. So far, Dean Arnold had managed to avoid the reporters, but she knew it was only a matter of time before they contacted university officials for comments about the party and the hospitalizations.

The incident could not have come at a worse time, or under worse circumstances. A student at another college in the state had died from alcohol poisoning just two weeks earlier, and national attention recently had been focused on alcohol-related deaths at other universities. One of the severely intoxicated MU students was the daughter of an MU trustee and prominent business leader in the state. Although the party was not sponsored by an MU fraternity, it had been held at a farmhouse rented by three members of one Greek-letter organization, and many of the party participants were affiliated with social fraternities and sororities. All three of the students who were hospitalized were under the age of twenty-one, and all had obtained alcohol at the party.

During the past three semesters, MU staff had implemented a series of educational programs about alcohol abuse, and several student groups had participated in activities such as Alcohol Awareness Week. Student affairs staff, including the vice chancellor for student affairs, the dean of students, the director of the counseling center, and the director of student judicial affairs, had used every opportunity to speak with students about responsible alcohol use. Resident assistants had done a reasonably good job of enforcing the university's prohibition against underage alcohol use in the residence halls, and the university had a lengthy policy intended to control the consumption of alcohol at events held on campus. Despite these efforts, results of the annual MU survey of alcohol and drug use indicated no significant decrease in students' alcohol consumption and, in fact, the proportion of students engaged in binge drinking seemed to be on the rise.

After finishing his conversation with Dean Arnold, Tom Gonzalez, the vice chancellor for student affairs, contacted the chancellor and the director of public affairs to alert them to the situation. Although the chancellor expressed support for the steps Tom outlined to deal with the party and its consequences, his expectations for a broader response were clearly stated: "I understand the difficulties involved in changing students' behavior and attitudes about alcohol. But we have a responsibility to our students, their parents, and the state. I have great confidence that you and your staff will find new and creative ways to address this problem. The bottom line is, I want you to fix it and to fix it soon." The chancellor also made it clear that he did not want to find himself in the middle of this particular controversy.

The chancellor asked for a detailed report on the party and its aftermath by Monday morning. He also requested a plan of action, to be completed by December 1, describing the process to be used to stop—or at least drastically reduce—excessive consumption of alcohol by MU students. After contemplating other career opportunities, Gonzalez called a Monday morning meeting of student affairs department heads to brief them on what had happened and to discuss how to respond to the chancellor's mandate. In the ensuing discussion, Gonzalez and his colleagues decided that if the principles of good practice for student affairs represented consensus about how to conduct the work of student affairs, they might be the most appropriate way to tackle this thorny problem.

Initiating a Response

The vice chancellor for student affairs recognized that alcohol abuse by students was an institutional problem and that many within the university had relevant information and expertise. With the help of the dean of students, the director of counseling, and the director of residence life, Gonzalez held a series of in-depth interviews and focus group discussions with university leaders, members of the health sciences faculty, leaders of a wide range of student organizations, local tavern owners, and members of the MU marketing and advertising department. His purpose in conducting these interviews was threefold: (1) to identify persons within the community who were willing and able to help design and implement a strategy to address the problem, (2) to begin to collect data about the nature of, and solutions for, the problem, and (3) to communicate commitment to an institution-wide effort to stop alcohol abuse.

The interviews took two weeks to complete, but the results of these discussions convinced Tom that there were many people willing to assist in dealing with the problem. Through this initial research, the interviewers also were able to begin to identify the range of issues that must be addressed.

At the same time, however, Gonzalez recognized that he had neither the time nor the expertise to devote his full attention to solving the campus alcohol problem. He approached his colleague, the MU provost, with a proposal: Gonzalez would use funds from vacant student affairs positions to buy the quarter-time release of two faculty members who would lead the development of a plan for the chancellor. One faculty member was from the health sciences department and had expert knowledge about alcohol use, abuse, and education. The second member of the faculty was in the marketing and advertising department and had expert knowledge about how to communicate ideas to students and the public. With the provost's approval and the faculty members' consent, a campus-wide task force on responsible alcohol use was created. The formation of the committee and its goals were widely publicized in the MU and local media, and the chancellor affirmed the university's support for developing healthy lifestyles, as well as the university's "zero tolerance" for irresponsible and illegal alcohol use.

Vice Chancellor Gonzalez and the two faculty members next turned to student organizations for assistance. They identified members of the Interfraternity Council, Panhellenic, black Greek organizations, the student government, and the student union board who were interested in, and had insightful comments about, addressing the quality of student life at MU—including alcohol use. To this group were added the dean of students, the assistant director of residence life, the director of student judicial affairs, the associate provost for undergraduate life, the associate deans for student services in the colleges of liberal arts and business administration, and the chair of the MU faculty senate. Gonzalez supplied the committee with secretarial support from his office and a budget that he and the provost had gathered from various funding sources.

At their first meeting, the committee members decided to organize themselves into teams, each of which was composed of at least one member of the student affairs staff, an academic administrator or faculty member, and students. Data collected in the focus group interviews were used to define directions for further research—the first phase of the committee's work. Those data revealed that MU students were well aware of laws regarding alcohol, as well as many of the health hazards of abuse, but they believed that drinking was inherent to college life, especially at MU, that most of their peers drank to excess without negative consequences, that alcohol was necessary to escape from the pressures of their lives as students, and that the university should not be concerned with their personal decisions about drinking. The committee decided to focus some of their efforts on identifying university standards and values about healthy lifestyles, alcohol use, and acceptable conduct in an academic community.

The two faculty committee chairs taught courses in which students were required to conduct research and design special projects. The marketing and advertising professor recruited five students to develop an advertising campaign about alcohol use and abuse among MU students; their first step was to assess what efforts had been effective at other universities. The health sciences professor devoted a portion of her graduate seminar in health education to the issue. Her students formed project teams to study alcohol use among MU students—when, how much, under what circumstances, by whom, and so on.

While the committee proceeded with its data collection, Tom Gonzalez asked his staff to review with students the alcohol policies and procedures found in the code of student conduct, the college bulletin, and the student handbooks. The review was intended to identify consistencies and inconsistencies in the rules and their enforcement, and to identify whether these codes and handbooks stated clearly the university stance regarding alcohol use and students' use of free time. He also asked that admissions and orientation programs and publications be examined to determine what messages the university conveyed about alcohol to prospective and new students.

After another two weeks had passed, Tom Gonzalez called a meeting of all who were involved with the alcohol project to discuss their progress. The following information emerged: Research by the faculty and students identified binge drinking as the primary alcohol problem for students at MU. Their data indicated that education alone would not change students' drinking behavior, and they did not find any research at other institutions that suggested that educational efforts to discourage students from drinking had any effect on behavior. However, they concluded that the best course of action at MU would be to focus on discouraging binge drinking through a campaign that (1) described the extent and consequences of the problem, (2) established a peer norm of support and challenge so that students would feel responsible for discouraging self-destructive behaviors among their friends and encouraging getting help to deal with problem drinking, and (3) communicated clear community values and expectations for healthy lifestyle choices. The study groups also had concluded that enforcement of policies against underage drinking should continue but that most staff efforts should be directed at the most destructive behaviors—binge drinking and its consequences (for example, drunk driving, date rape, academic failure).

The student representatives on the committee had reached the same conclusion. They had conducted extensive and intensive conversations with a wide range of MU students, seeking honest and open insights about how students made decisions about alcohol use, how they viewed their peers' decisions, and what they thought the university expected of them. The student representatives concluded that a series of programs directed at (1) helping students discuss, set, and enforce community norms for acceptable behavior and (2) creating peer networks of support was much more likely to be successful at changing problem behaviors than trying to prohibit activities students saw as an essential component of college life. To achieve these goals, however, cooperation among student groups would be necessary—not an insignificant challenge. Divisions between members of predominantly white and predominantly black Greek organizations were deep, based on lack of communication and un-examined stereotypes. Rifts and suspicion between Greeks and non-Greeks were even greater.

The student and academic affairs staff generally agreed with the students' recommendations. They were particularly concerned that institutional community members had not done a good job of communicating their expectations of students regarding alcohol. Although there were prohibitions against underage drinking in the code of student conduct, student handbook, and the residence life handbook, these publications did not include statements encouraging good decisions about recreation, friends, diet, sleep, and drug use (including alcohol). Nor were students of legal age discouraged from drinking to excess. None of these topics were addressed in admissions or orientation programs. All in all, although some general references were made to alcohol use in institutional policy statements, very little time or effort was devoted to informing students of what was expected of them as members of an academic community.

During this discussion, questions arose concerning activities that had become traditions at the institution. One such tradition was the annual Block Party held in an open field owned by the university the first Thursday prior to the start of classes each fall semester. Students brought coolers of beer, and one or more fraternities sponsored a disc jockey or band. Thousands of students attended, and it had come to be an important way for new students to meet returning students and for returning students to become reacquainted after summer vacation. Alums recalled Block Party as one of the highlights of their time at MU. Despite the positive social benefits of the event, however, excessive alcohol consumption seemed to be its primary focus.

About six years ago, community and police concerns about Block Party (for example, drunk driving arrests, noise, vandalism, emergency treatment for alcohol overdoses) led MU leaders to assume institutional responsibility for organizing the event. Buses were provided to transport people to and from the party to eliminate driving under the influence, and staff developed a system for carding students bringing alcohol to the event to ensure that they were of legal age. Staff also set a limit on the amount of alcohol any one person could bring to the party: no more than a six-pack of beer. And the university provided appropriate security and medical assistance. In spite of these precautions, excessive and underage drinking were common at the event.

A second MU "tradition" also was examined. The weekend before finals in the spring semester, IFC and Panhellenic jointly sponsored a spring-fling beer keg roll and afternoon concert in a playing field adjacent to the football stadium. Alcohol was permitted, and a system similar to that for Block Party was used for carding students. Again, student affairs personnel were involved in helping control the event and, again, students viewed excessive alcohol use as an acceptable aspect of the "tradition."

The work of the study committees raised obvious questions: What messages did these events convey to students about acceptable alcohol use? What messages did they communicate about the community's expectations for student life at MU? What role did these events play in encouraging a campus culture of drinking and partying that was detrimental to students? New students were, for all intents and purposes, introduced to student life by the annual Block Party. The academic year at MU began and ended with a large university-sponsored drinking event.

Intervention Strategy

The following decisions were made as a result of the research and discussions conducted in the first month of the project:

1. A budget was established for a class project in marketing and advertising to develop an anti-binge-drinking campaign. The money would come from the university's foundation and excess revenue from washer and dryer receipts in the residence halls. Information to be contained on the printed materials would come, in part, from the faculty and students in health sciences. Student groups would be involved in evaluating the advertising campaign

as it was developed. This research would be finished, and the campaign implemented, by the end of the fall semester. The campaign would include posters, radio spots, newspaper articles, and a short video that would run prior to campus movies.

2. Orientation programs would be changed to include a series of vignettes about alcohol misuse and other social issues students confronted in college. Students from the theater department, with the help of the theater faculty, would design the scenarios as part of summer orientation. Also, orientation leaders would be instructed on the university's alcohol policies and would have conversations with students about alcohol misuse, particularly the negative effects of binge drinking. The admissions office would integrate information about alcohol use and expectations for student behavior in all materials provided to prospective students; these publications would emphasize the centrality of the educational mission of MU.

3. The chancellor would use part of his speech welcoming the community back for the new year to set expectations for behavior. He would emphasize the mission of the institution to build educated citizens who could be responsible for their own actions and to create a supportive community of learning consistent with the values and ethics of the institution.

4. To determine the effects of the activities that would be undertaken, the director of student life research would conduct standardized pre- and posttests to measure students' alcohol knowledge, consumption, and binge-drinking behavior. The baseline data would be gathered during the fall semester, and subsequent data would be gathered each year. A second measure of behavioral change would include the number of alcohol violations reported to the office of student judicial affairs, damage in residence halls, and reports of alcohol-related problems obtained from the offices of residence life, office of student judicial affairs, and the campus police department.

5. The university would stop sponsoring the Block Party and the keg roll. Instead, the university would offer in the fall semester an event to be called "First Night" in which the university would supply free nonalcoholic beverages, bands, and a variety of carnival-

type activities free of charge to all students. This would be located where Block Party had been held and also would be open to all students without charge. In the spring the university would sponsor a concert by well-known groups to replace the spring fling. Both events would be cosponsored by the Interfraternity Council, Student Government Association, Panhellenic Council, Black Student Association, and the student union, and a steering committee of representatives of all these groups would coordinate planning and implementation. These changes were publicized as part of a campus-wide effort to reinforce the values of MU as a learning community. In writing and in person, faculty, staff, and others emphasized academic potential and high expectations for achievement of MU students, the excellence of the faculty and staff, and the community's commitment to helping all MU students be successful.

6. A peer network of alcohol educators was formed to help student communities and groups (for example, fraternity and sorority chapters, residence hall floors, student government committees) form and implement norms and expectations regarding alcohol use that were consistent with university values, as well as to provide educational programs and problem solving as requested by student organizations.

7. The "alcohol committee"—as it had come to be known—would continue to coordinate campus-wide efforts to integrate healthy decision making about alcohol use into the curriculum, out-of-class programs and services, and university publications. Although binge drinking would be the committee's primary focus for the time being, they hoped to be able to turn their attention to broader issues of wellness in the future.

Analysis

This case study offers an example of using all of the principles of good practice to address a campus problem. In confronting excessive alcohol use at Midwest University, Vice Chancellor Gonzalez and his colleagues did the following:

• Engaged students in active learning: At all stages of the effort, students were involved in collective decision making on educational issues and had the opportunity to work with faculty to develop and implement interventions. Equally important, student opinions and experiences informed decisions about what actions to take (for example, focusing on problems associated with binge drinking) and not to take (for example, prohibiting all alcohol use). Students also were able to apply classroom learning to a real-world problem. An advertising and marketing campaign to prevent binge drinking gave the faculty member and the students first-hand experience in negotiating contracts, working with vendors, and using focus groups. The health sciences students had similar opportunities. Their research on what worked to stem binge drinking and what did not informed marketing and advertising decisions. Together they had an opportunity to apply knowledge and skills from two fields—advertising and health education—in service to their peers.

• Helped students develop coherent values and ethical standards: A review of university policies in the code of student conduct, college bulletin, student handbook, and residence life handbook emphasized the need for explicit statements about expectations and values, and revealed the problems posed by inconsistent messages about alcohol. This review, coupled with policy analysis, resulted in the university's decision to alter the Block Party and the keg roll, two events that were inconsistent with the university's commitment to discourage underage drinking and prevent binge drinking. Also, beginning each year with statements from the chancellor about "what it means to be a member of the MU community" contributed to students' understanding of the values and ethical standards of the institution.

• Set and communicated high expectations for learning: One of the foci for the anti-binge-drinking campaign was emphasizing how excessive consumption of alcohol detracts from learning. The chancellor's statements, orientation experiences, and admissions publications set high expectations for students by challenging them to fulfill their potential as learners and to avoid behaviors that violate the history and traditions of the campus. The chancellor reminded students that the institution had a history of developing educated citizens and that certain behaviors detracted from the high expectations.

• Used systematic inquiry to improve student and institutional performance: Data—from institutional research and research from other sources—informed the entire process. The vice chancellor used focus groups early on to help identify and define the problem. He went to the health science faculty for their knowledge about alcohol use and abuse. The director of student life and learning research used pre-post test design to determine whether the new initiatives had any effect on student behavior. Other sources of information also were included in assessing the impact of the project, such as data from residence life, student discipline, and the police.

• Used resources effectively to achieve the institutional mission and goals: One of the missions of the institution was to educate responsible citizens. A second was to ensure the safety of students on campus. Binge drinking and some of the activities that the institution had promoted (for example, Block Party) were antithetical to these goals. The vice chancellor was able to marshal student affairs resources from unused money in various accounts and from lapsed salaries from vacant positions, and to obtain assistance from the provost. He also sought money from the institution's foundation, which provided him with a grant to assist with the implementation of the advertising campaign. More important than the sources of the funds, however, is their use to further the institution's educational mission.

• Forged educational partnerships that advance student learning: From the beginning, the vice chancellor involved members from all parts of the university community, including faculty and students. He sought advice from faculty experts in health sciences and from the marketing and advertising departments. Later, the faculty, using class time and resources directed at solving a real-life problem, furthered the notion of partnerships by putting students to work on an issue about which they were familiar and interested. These and other efforts affirmed the impact of binge drinking on the entire community and reinforced the importance of a community response to the problem.

• Built supportive and inclusive communities: Although this project was not directed at what one might ordinarily think of as issues of difference, an important aspect of making it work was promoting communication across student organizations and within the student body as a whole. Community members recognized early on that an effective campaign to prevent binge drinking needed to focus on peer support and, therefore, peer communication. This approach encouraged a sense of community—and community responsibility—among students. Also, from the beginning, participants from all aspects of the MU community were engaged in addressing and solving the problem.

Postscript

Because this case study is based, in part, on the experience of an actual university, a postscript—that is, what happened as a result of all this—is warranted. The campaign developed by the faculty and students was comprehensive. Posters created by design students and incorporating photographs taken by photography students were displayed in the residence halls; new posters were hung each month. A student staff member on the campus newspaper wrote fifteen short stories about alcohol use and binge drinking, which ran as a series of articles. Ten one-minute radio spots were developed by students in the marketing and advertising program, and students from the campus radio station produced them at no cost. These one-minute spots included comments by the chancellor, student leaders, and the police chief, but most featured students' concerns about binge drinking.

The director of orientation, in collaboration with the theater department, developed a series of vignettes about binge drinking and other campus issues. These vignettes were incorporated into orientation; new students were asked to think about and respond to the situations dramatized. Also, students were advised by their orientation leaders about issues regarding drinking on campus (for example, rules, making good choices). The chancellor delivered his remarks, as agreed, at the opening convocation.

Block Party was canceled and First Night was held in its place. Student reaction was mixed. Freshmen enjoyed the experience, but few returning students attended. The spring event was canceled due to rain, but the scheduled bands played in the institution's convocation center to large and enthusiastic crowds.

After one year of initiatives, students were surveyed about their drinking behavior. Results showed that the percentage of students consuming alcohol was unchanged since the previous survey, and about the same percentage of students (87 percent) reported that they had consumed alcohol at least once within thirty days of completing the survey. However, both the frequency of drinking and the amount of consumption per student at one sitting declined by 25 and 34 percent, respectively. Damage in the residence halls decreased a small amount (by approximately $3,000), but alcohol-related violations declined by 33 percent. Focus groups conducted to ascertain the effects of the initiatives found that most students knew something about the campaign, felt generally positive about the approach, and reported that excessive alcohol consumption was generally frowned on and considered immature by most of their friends. And in that year the university had only one serious alcohol-related problem—a student had taken barbiturates while drinking, in what might have been an attempted suicide.

Concluding Remarks

The principles of good practice for student affairs are intended to build consensus on the actions associated with creating high-quality undergraduate experiences, thereby reinforcing a common agenda for student affairs—fostering student learning. We believe that without this agenda, student affairs is hampered in its ability to meet its challenges successfully. The principles are designed to be incorporated into our daily work and to shape how we think about our responsibilities, communicate our purposes, and interact with students. They also are intended as a guide for assessing our contributions to student learning, and for examining and implementing our missions, policies, programs, and services. Most important, however, is their potential for engaging all of us in ongoing dialogue about the purposes of our work and how those purposes can and should be achieved.

Appendix:

Principles of Good Practice
for Student Affairs

Good practice in student affairs

1. Engages students in active learning

2. Helps students develop coherent values and ethical standards

3. Sets and communicates high expectations for student learning

4. Uses systematic inquiry to improve student and institutional performance

5. Uses resources effectively to achieve institutional missions and goals

6. Forges educational partnerships that advance student learning

7. Builds supportive and inclusive communities

   1. *Good practice in student affairs engages students in active learning*. Active learning invites students to bring their life experiences

---

into the learning process, reflect on their own and others' perspectives as they expand their viewpoints, and apply new understandings to their own lives. Good student affairs practice provides students with opportunities for experimentation through programs focused on engaging students in various learning experiences. These opportunities include experiential learning such as student government; collective decision making on educational issues; field-based learning such as internships; peer instruction; and structured group experiences such as community service, international study, and resident advising.

2. *Good practice in student affairs helps students develop coherent values and ethical standards*. Good student affairs practice provides opportunities for students, faculty, staff, and student affairs educators to demonstrate the values that define a learning community. Effective learning communities are committed to justice, honesty, equality, civility, freedom, dignity, and responsible citizenship. Such communities challenge students to develop meaningful values for a life of learning. Standards espoused by student affairs divisions should reflect the values that bind the campus community to its educational mission.

3. *Good practice in student affairs sets and communicates high expectations for learning*. Student learning is enhanced when expectations for student performance inside and outside the classroom are high, appropriate to students' abilities and aspirations, and consistent with the institution's mission and philosophy. Expectations should address the wide range of student behaviors associated with academic achievement, intellectual and psychosocial development, and individual and community responsibility. Good student affairs divisions systematically describe desired levels of performance to students as well as to practitioners and regularly assess whether their performances are consistent with institutional expectations.

4. *Good practice in student affairs uses systematic inquiry to improve student and institutional performance*. Good practice in student affairs occurs when student affairs educators ask, "What are students learn-

ing from our programs and services, and how can their learning be enhanced?" Knowledge of and ability to analyze research about students and their learning are critical components of good student affairs practice. Student affairs educators who are skilled in using assessment methods acquire high-quality information; effective application of this information to practice results in programs and change strategies that improve institutional and student achievement.

5. *Good practice in student affairs uses resources effectively to achieve institutional missions and goals*. Effective student affairs divisions are responsible stewards of their institutions' financial and human resources. They use principles of organizational planning to create and improve learning environments throughout the campus that emphasize institutions' desired educational outcomes for students. Because the most important resources for learning are human resources, good student affairs divisions involve professionals who can translate into practice guiding theories and research from areas such as human development, learning and cognition, communication, leadership, and program design and implementation.

6. *Good practice in student affairs forges educational partnerships that advance student learning*. Good student affairs practice initiates educational partnerships and develops structures that support collaboration. Partners for learning include students, faculty, academic administrators, staff, and others inside and outside the institution. Collaboration involves all aspects of the community in the development and implementation of institutional goals and reminds participants of their common commitment to students and their learning. Relationships forged across departments and divisions demonstrate a healthy institutional approach to learning by fostering inclusiveness, bringing multiple perspectives to bear on problems, and affirming shared educational values.

7. *Good practice in student affairs builds supportive and inclusive communities*. Student learning occurs best in communities that value diversity, promote social responsibility, encourage discussion and debate, recognize accomplishments, and foster a sense of belonging

among their members. Good student affairs practice cultivates supportive environments by encouraging connections among students, faculty, and student affairs practitioners. This interweaving of students' academic, interpersonal, and developmental experiences is a critical institutional role for student affairs.

Principles of Good Practice Study Group

In 1996 Paul Oliaro, president of the American College Personnel Association (ACPA), and Suzanne Gordon, president of the National Association of Student Personnel Administrators (NASPA), appointed a study group to draft *Principles of Good Practice for Student Affairs*. Members of the study group included Gregory Blimling (co-chair, Appalachian State University), Elizabeth Whitt (co-chair, University of Iowa), Marcia Baxter Magolda (Miami University), Arthur Chickering (Vermont College, Norwich University), Johnetta Cross Brazzell (Spelman College), Jon Dalton (Florida State University), Zelda Gamson (University of Massachusetts), George Kuh (Indiana University), Ernest Pascarella (University of Iowa), Linda Reisser (Suffolk County Community College), Larry Roper (Oregon State University), and Charles Schroeder (University of Missouri-Columbia).

References

Allen, K. E., & Garb, E. L. (1993). Reinventing student affairs: Something old and something new. *NASPA Journal, 30,* 93–100.

Allen, W. (1987, May/June). Black colleges vs. White colleges: The fork in the road for Black students. *Change, 19,* 28–34.

American Association for Higher Education. (1992). *Principles of good practice for assessing student learning.* Washington, DC: Author.

American College Personnel Association. (1990). Statement of principles and standards. *Journal of College Student Personnel, 31,* 197–202.

American College Personnel Association. (1994). *The student learning imperative: Implications for student affairs.* Washington, DC: Author.

American College Personnel Association. (1998). *Senior scholar essays: Senior scholar trends analysis project.* Washington, DC: Author.

American College Personnel Association and National Association of Student Personnel Administrators. (1997). *Principles of good practice for student affairs.* Washington, DC: Authors.

American Council on Education. (1937). *The student personnel point of view: A report of a conference on the philosophy and development of student personnel work in colleges and universities* (American Council on Education Study, Series 1, Vol. 1, No. 3). Washington, DC: Author.

American Council on Education. (1949). *The student personnel point of view.* Washington, DC: Author.

Andreas, R. A. (1991). Where achievement is the rule: The case of Xavier University of Louisiana. In G. D. Kuh & J. H. Schuh (Eds.), *The role and contributions of student affairs in involving colleges* (pp. 97–114). Washington, DC: National Association of Student Personnel Administrators.

Angelo, T. A., & Cross, K. P. (1993). *Classroom assessment techniques: A handbook for college teachers* (2nd ed.). San Francisco: Jossey-Bass.

Association of American Colleges. (1991). *Liberal learning and the arts and sciences major (Vol. 1): The challenge of connecting learning.* Washington, DC: Author.

Astin, A. (1991). *Assessment for excellence: The philosophy and practice of assessment and evaluation in higher education.* New York: ACE/Macmillan.

Astin, A. (1993). *What matters in college? Four critical years revisited.* San Francisco: Jossey-Bass.

Astin, A. (1996). Involvement in learning revisited: Lessons we have learned. *Journal of College Student Development, 37,* 123–133.

Astin, A. (1998). The changing American college student: Thirty-year trends, 1966–1996. *Review of Higher Education, 21,* 115–136.

Astin, A., Green, K. E., & Korn, W. (1987). *The American freshman: Twenty-year trends (1966–1985).* Los Angeles: University of California, Higher Education Research Institute.

Banning, J. H. (1989). Creating a climate for successful student development: The campus ecology manager role. In U. Delworth & G. Hanson (Eds.), *Student services: A handbook for the profession* (pp. 304–322). San Francisco: Jossey-Bass.

Banta, T. W., & Associates (1993). *Making a difference: Outcomes of a decade of assessment in higher education.* San Francisco: Jossey-Bass.

Banta, T. W., Lund, J. P., Black, K. E., & Oblander, F. W. (1996). *Assessment in practice: Putting principles to work on college campuses.* San Francisco: Jossey-Bass.

Barr, M. J., & Associates (1993). *The handbook of student affairs administration.* San Francisco: Jossey-Bass.

Barr, R. B., & Tagg, J. (1995, November/December). From teaching to learning: A new paradigm for undergraduate education. *Change, 27,* 13–25.

Baxter Magolda, M. B. (1992). *Knowing and reasoning in college: Gender-related patterns in students' intellectual development.* San Francisco: Jossey-Bass.

Baxter Magolda, M. B. (1997). Facilitating meaningful dialogues about race. *About Campus, 2*(5), 14–18.

Beeler, K. J., & Hunter, D. E. (1991). The promise of student affairs research. In K. J. Beeler & D. E. Hunter (Eds.), *Puzzles and pieces in wonderland: The promise and practice of student affairs research* (pp. 1–17). Washington, DC: National Association of Student Personnel Administrators.

Belenky, M., Clinchy, B., Goldberger, N., & Tarule, J. (1986). *Women's ways of knowing: The development of self, voice, and mind.* New York: Basic Books.

Benedict, L. G. (1991). In search of the lost chord: Applying research to planning and decision-making. In K. J. Beeler & D. E. Hunter (Eds.), *Puzzles and pieces in wonderland: The promise and practice of student affairs research* (pp. 18–34). Washington, DC: National Association of Student Personnel Administrators.

Bennett, M. J. (1986). A developmental approach to training for intercultural sensitivity. *International Journal of Intercultural Relations, 10,* 179–196.

Bensimon, E. M., & Neumann, A. (1993). *Redesigning collegiate leadership: Teams and teamwork in higher education.* Baltimore: The Johns Hopkins University Press.

Bernstein, N. (1996, May 5). With colleges holding court, discretion vies with fairness. *The New York Times,* p. 16.

Blake, E. S. (1979, September). Classroom and context: An educational dialectic. *Academe, 65,* 280–292.

Blake, E. S. (1996, September/October). The yin and yang of student learning in college. *About Campus, 1,* 4–9.

Blake, J. H., Evenbeck, S. E., & Melodia, A. (1997, March/April). Holding students to high expectations is everybody's business. *About Campus, 2,* 31–32.

Blimling, G. S. (1993). The influence of college residence halls on students. In J. Smart (Ed.), *Higher education: Handbook of theory and research* (Vol. 9, pp. 248–307). New York: Agathon.

Blimling, G. S., & Alschuler, A. S. (1996). Creating a home for the spirit of learning: Contributions of student development educators. *Journal of College Student Development, 37,* 203–316.

Blocher, D. H. (1978). Campus learning environments and the ecology of student development. In J. H. Banning (Ed.), *Campus ecology: A perspective for student affairs* (pp. 17–23). Washington, DC: National Association of Student Personnel Administrators.

Bloland, P. A., Stamatakos, L. C., & Rogers, R. R. (1994). *Reform in student affairs: A critique of student development.* Greensboro, NC: ERIC Counseling and Student Services Clearinghouse.

Bloland, P. A., Stamatakos, L. C., & Rogers, R. R. (1996). Redirecting the role of student affairs to focus on student learning. *Journal of College Student Development, 37,* 217–226.

Blystone, C., Conlon, M., Kooker, D., Marriner, N., & Wigton, K. (1996, November). *Resident Assistant Institute: Past traditions and new directions for RA training.* Presentation at the Great Lakes Association of College and University Housing Officers Conference, Perrysburg, OH.

Bohr, L., Pascarella, E. T., Nora, A., & Terenzini, P. T. (1995). Do black students learn more at historically black or predominantly white colleges? *Journal of College Student Development, 36,* 75–85.

Bonser, C. F. (1992). Total quality education. *Public Administration Review, 52*, 504–512.

Boyer, E. L. (1987). *The undergraduate experience in America.* New York: Harper & Row.

Boyer, E. L. (1990). *Campus life: In search of community.* Princeton, NJ: Carnegie Foundation for the Advancement of Teaching.

Boyer Commission on Educating Undergraduates in the Research University. (1998). *Reinventing undergraduate education: A blueprint for America's research Universities.* Stony Brook, NY: State University of New York.

Brown, J. S. (1997, January/February). On becoming a learning organization. *About Campus, 1*, 5–10.

Brown, R. D. (1972). *Student development in tomorrow's higher education: A return to the academy* (Student Personnel Series No. 16). Washington, DC: American College Personnel Association.

Brown, R. D. (1986). Research: A frill or an obligation? *Journal of College Student Personnel, 27*(3), 195.

Brown, R. D. (1991). Student affairs research on trial. In K. J. Beeler & D. E. Hunter (Eds.), *Puzzles and pieces in wonderland: The promise and practice of student affairs research* (pp. 124–142). Washington, DC: National Association of Student Personnel Administrators.

Calvert, G. (1993). *High-wire management: Risk-taking tactics for leaders, innovators, and trailblazers.* San Francisco: Jossey-Bass.

Cantor, N., & Mischel, W. (1977). Traits as prototypes: Effects on recognition memory. *Journal of Personality and Social Psychology, 35*, 38–48.

Caple, R. B. (1996). The learning debate: A historical perspective. *Journal of College Student Development, 37*, 193–202.

Carnegie Council on Policy Studies in Higher Education. (1980). *Three thousand futures: The next 20 years for higher education.* San Francisco: Jossey-Bass.

Carnegie Foundation for the Advancement of Teaching. (1990). *Campus life: In search of community.* Princeton, NJ: Princeton University Press.

Chickering, A. W., & Gamson, Z. F. (1987a). *Principles of good practice for undergraduate education* [Special insert to Wingspread Journal (June 1987)]. Racine, WI: Johnson Foundation.

Chickering, A. W., & Gamson, Z. F. (1987b). Seven principles for good practice in undergraduate education. *AAHE Bulletin, 39*(7), 3–7.

Chickering, A. W., & Reisser, L. (1993). *Education and identity* (2nd ed.). San Francisco: Jossey-Bass.

Coate, L. E. (1990). TQM on campus: Implementing Total Quality Management in a university setting. *NACUBO Business Officer, 26*, 26–35.

Corts, T. E. (1997, March/April). Total quality at Samford University. *About Campus, 2*, 11–15.

Cotter, M. (1996). Systems-thinking in a knowledge-creating organization. *Journal of Innovative Management, 2*(1), 15–30.

Covey, S. R. (1990). *Principle-centered leadership.* New York: Simon & Schuster.

Cross, K. P. (1996). New lenses on learning. *About Campus, 1*(1), 4–9.

Cuming, P. (1981). *The power handbook: A strategic guide to organizational and personal effectiveness.* New York: Van Nostrand Reinhold Co., Inc.

Dalton, J. C. (1996). Managing human resources. In S. R. Komives & D. B. Woodard, Jr. (Eds.), *Student services: A handbook for the profession* (pp. 494–512). San Francisco: Jossey-Bass.

Deming, W. E. (1993). *The new economics for industry, government, and education.* Cambridge, MA: Massachusetts Institute of Technology, Center for Advanced Engineering Study.

Dewey, J. (1916). *Democracy and education.* New York: The Free Press.

Dewey, J. (1950). *Reconstruction in philosophy.* New York: American Library.

Dungee, G. J. (1996). *Restructuring in higher education and endless speculation on the state of student affairs.* Unpublished manuscript, National Association of Student Personnel Administrators.

Dyer, W. G. (1995). *Team building: Current issues and new alternatives* (3rd ed.). Reading, MA: Addison-Wesley.

Education Commission of the States. (1995). *Making quality count in undergraduate education.* Denver, CO: Author.

Ender, S. C., Newton, F. B., & Caple, R. B. (1996). Contributions to learning: Present realities. In S. C. Ender, F. B. Newton, & R. B. Caple (Eds.), *Contributing to learning: The role of student affairs* (pp. 5–17). San Francisco: Jossey-Bass.

Engstrom, C. M., & Tinto, V. (1997, July/August). Working together for service learning. *About Campus, 2*, 10–15.

Ern, E. H. (1993). Managing resources strategically. In M. J. Barr & Associates (Eds.), *The handbook of student affairs administration* (pp. 439–454). San Francisco: Jossey-Bass.

Erwin, T. D. (1991). *Assessing student learning and development.* San Francisco: Jossey-Bass.

Erwin, T. D. (1996). Assessment, evaluation, and research. In S. R. Komives, D. B. Woodard, & Associates (Eds.), *Student services: A handbook for the profession.* (3rd ed., pp. 415–434). San Francisco: Jossey-Bass.

Ewell, P. T. (Ed.). (1985). *Assessing educational outcomes.* (New Directions for Institutional Research No. 47). San Francisco: Jossey-Bass.

Ewell, P. T., & Jones, D. P. (1996). *Indicators of "good practice" in undergraduate education: A handbook for development and implementation*. Boulder, CO: National Center for Higher Education Management Systems.

Feldman, K. A., & Newcomb, T. M. (1969). *The impact of college on students: Vol. 1: An analysis of four decades of research*. San Francisco: Jossey-Bass.

Fleming, J. (1984). *Blacks in college: A comparative study of students' success in black and in white institutions*. San Francisco: Jossey-Bass.

Freire, P. (1986). *Pedagogy of the oppressed* (M. Bergman Ramos, Trans.). New York: Continuum. (Original work published 1970.)

Friedlander, J., Murrell, P. H., & MacDougall, P. R. (1993). The community college student experiences questionnaire. In T. W. Banta & Associates (Eds.), *Making a difference: Outcomes of a decade of assessment in higher education* (pp. 196–210). San Francisco: Jossey-Bass.

Funk and Wagnalls Standard College Dictionary. (1966). New York: Funk and Wagnalls.

Garvin, D. A. (1993). Building a learning organization. *Harvard Business Review, 71*(4), 78–91.

Gilligan, C. (1982). *In another voice*. Cambridge: Harvard University Press.

Gose, B. (1998, October 16). Average tuition rises 4 percent in a year, more than twice the rate of inflation. *The Chronicle of Higher Education*, p. A56.

Guskin, A. E. (1994a, July/August). Reducing student costs and enhancing student learning (Part I): Restructuring the administration. *Change, 26*, 22–29.

Guskin, A. E. (1994b, September/October). Reducing student costs and enhancing student learning (Part II): Restructuring the role of faculty. *Change, 26*, 16–25.

Guskin, A. E. (1997). Learning more, spending less. *About Campus, 2*, 4–9.

Hanson, G. (1991). The call to assessment: What role for student affairs? In K. J. Beeler & D. E. Hunter (Eds.), *Puzzles and pieces in wonderland: The promise and practice of student affairs research* (pp. 80–105). Washington, DC: National Association of Student Personnel Administrators.

Haworth, J. G. (1997, September/October). The misrepresentation of Generation X. *About Campus, 2*, 10–15.

Heath, D. (1968). *Growing up in college*. San Francisco: Jossey-Bass.

Hersey, P., & Blanchard, K. (1982). *Management of organizational behavior: Utilizing human resources*. Englewood Cliffs, NJ: Prentice Hall, Inc.

Hersh, R. H., Mills, J. P., & Fielding, G. D. (Eds.). (1980). *Models of moral education: An appraisal*. Reading, MA: Longman, Inc.

Hispanic Association of Colleges and Universities. (1991). *Annual report*. San Antonio, TX: Author.

Horowitz, H. L. (1984). *Alma mater: Design and experience in the women's colleges from their 19th Century beginnings to the 1930s.* New York: Knopf.

Horowitz, H. L. (1987). *Campus life: Undergraduate culture from the end of the 18th Century to the present.* New York: Knopf.

Hossler, D., Bean, J. P., & Associates (1990). *The strategic management of college enrollments.* San Francisco: Jossey-Bass.

Hossler, D., Schmit, J., & Vesper, N. (in press). *Going to college: Family, social, and educational influences on postsecondary decision-making.* Baltimore: The Johns Hopkins University Press.

Ivey, A. (1988). *Intentional interviewing and counseling* (2nd ed.). Belmont, CA: Wadsworth.

Jones, D., Dolence, M., & Phipps, R. (1998, May). New institutional and programmic configurations. In V. McMillan (Chair), *Technology and its ramifications for data systems: Report of the Policy Panel on Technology* (pp. 11–14). Washington, DC: U.S. Department of Education, National Center for Education Statistics.

Jussim, L. (1986). Self-fulfilling prophecies: A theoretical and integrative review. *Psychological Review, 93,* 429–445.

Kalsbeek, D. H. (1994). New perspectives for assessing the residential experience. In C. Schroeder & P. Mable (Eds.), *Realizing the educational potential of residence halls* (pp. 269–297). San Francisco: Jossey-Bass.

Kegan, R. (1993). Minding the curriculum: Of student epistemology and faculty conspiracy. In A. Garrod (Ed.), *Approaches to moral development: New research and emerging themes* (pp. 72–88). New York: Teachers College Press.

Kegan, R. (1994). *In over our heads: The mental demands of modern life.* Cambridge, MA: Harvard University Press.

Keller, G. (1985, January/February). Trees without fruit: The problem with research about higher education. *Change, 17,* 7–10.

King, P. M. (1994). Theories of college student development: Sequences and consequences. *Journal of College Student Development, 35,* 413–421.

King, P. M., & Kitchener, K. S. (1994). *Developing reflective judgment: Understanding and promoting intellectual growth and critical thinking in adolescents and adults.* San Francisco: Jossey-Bass.

Kinnick, M. K. (1985). Increasing the use of student outcomes information. In P. T. Ewell (Ed.), *Assessing educational outcomes* (New Directions for Institutional Research No. 47, pp. 93–109). San Francisco: Jossey-Bass.

Kirby, D. J. (1991, February). Dreaming ambitious dreams: The LeMoyne College values program. *AAHE Bulletin, 9,* 12–16.

Kohlberg, L. (1984). *The psychology of moral development: Essays on moral development* (Vol. 2). San Francisco: Harper and Row.

Komives, S. R., & Woodward, D. B., Jr. (1996). Building on the past, shaping the future. In S. R. Komives & D. B. Woodward, Jr. (Eds.), *Student services: A handbook for the profession* (3rd ed., pp. 536–555). San Francisco: Jossey-Bass.

Kotter, J. P. (1996). *Leading change.* Boston: Harvard Business School Press.

Krehbiel, L., & Strange, C. C. (1991). Checking of the truth: The case of Earlham College. In G. D. Kuh & J. H. Schuh (Eds.), *The role and contributions of student affairs in involving colleges* (pp. 148–16). Washington, DC: National Association of Student Personnel Administrators.

Kuh, G. D. (1990). Assessing student cultures. In W. G. Tierney (Ed.), *Assessing academic climates and cultures* (New Directions for Institutional Research No. 68, pp. 47–60). San Francisco: Jossey-Bass.

Kuh, G. D. (1991a). Caretakers of the collegiate culture: Student affairs at Stanford University. In G. D. Kuh & J. H. Schuh (Eds.), *The role and contributions of student affairs in involving colleges* (pp. 46–66). Washington, DC: National Association of Student Personnel Administrators.

Kuh, G. D. (1991b). Rethinking research in student affairs. In K. J. Beeler & D. E. Hunter (Eds.), *Puzzles and pieces in wonderland: The promise and practice of student affairs research* (pp. 55–79). Washington, DC: National Association of Student Personnel Administrators.

Kuh, G. D. (1993a). Assessing campus environments. In M. J. Barr & Associates (Eds.), *The handbook of student affairs administration* (pp. 30–48). San Francisco: Jossey-Bass.

Kuh, G. D. (1993b). Ethos: Its influence on student learning. *Liberal Education, 79* (4), 22–31.

Kuh, G. D. (1993c). In their own words: What students learn outside the classroom. *American Educational Research Journal, 30,* 277–304.

Kuh, G. D. (1995). The other curriculum: Out-of-class experiences associated with student learning and personal development. *Journal of Higher Education, 66,* 123–155.

Kuh, G. D. (1996a). Guiding principles for creating seamless learning environments for undergraduates. *Journal of College Student Development, 37,* 135–148.

Kuh, G. D. (1996b). Organizational theory. In S. R. Komives and D. B. Woodard, Jr. (Eds.), *Student services: A handbook for the profession* (pp. 269–294). San Francisco: Jossey-Bass.

Kuh, G. D. (1997a, June). *Working together to enhance student learning inside and outside the classroom.* Paper presented at the annual AAHE Assessment and Quality Conference, Miami, FL.

Kuh, G. D. (1997b, November). *How are we doing? Tracking the quality of the undergraduate experience from the 1960s to the present.* Paper presented at the Association for the Study of Higher Education Conference, Albuquerque, NM.

Kuh, G. D. (1997c, September/)October). You gotta' believe. *About Campus, 2,* 2–3.

Kuh, G. D., & Andreas, R. E. (1991). It's about time: Using qualitative methods in student life studies. *Journal of College Student Development, 32,* 397–405.

Kuh, G. D., Bean, J. P., Bradley, R. K., & Coomes, M. D. (1986). Is one galaxy enough? *Journal of College Student Personnel, 27,* 311–312.

Kuh, G. D., Branch Douglas, K., Lund, J. P., & Ramin-Gyurnek, J. (1994). *Student learning outside the classroom: Transcending artificial boundaries* (ASHE-ERIC Higher Education Report No. 8). Washington, DC: George Washington University, School of Education and Human Development.

Kuh, G., Lyons, J., Miller, T., & Trow, J. A. (1994). *Reasonable expectations: Renewing the educational compact between institutions and students.* Washington, DC: National Association of Student Personnel Administrators.

Kuh, G. D., Miller, T., Lyons, J., & Trow, J. (1995). *Reasonable expectations.* Washington, DC: National Association of Student Personnel Administrators.

Kuh, G. D., Schuh, J. H., Whitt, E. J., & Associates. (1991). *Involving colleges: Successful approaches to fostering student learning and development outside the classroom.* San Francisco: Jossey-Bass.

Kuh, G. D., & Vesper, N. (1997). A comparison of student experiences with good practices in undergraduate education between 1990 and 1994. *Review of Higher Education, 21,* 43–61.

Kuh, G. D, Vesper, N., Connolly, M. R., & Pace, C. R. (1997). *College Student Experiences Questionnaire: Revised norms for the 3rd edition.* Bloomington, IN: Indiana University, School of Education, Center for Postsecondary Research and Planning.

Kuh, G. D., Vesper, N., & Pace, C. R. (1997). Using process indicators to estimate student gains associated with good practices in undergraduate education. *Research in Higher Education, 38,* 435–454.

Larson, C. E. and La Fasto, F. M. (1989). *Teamwork: What must go right/what can go wrong.* Newbury Park, CA: SAGE Publications, Inc.

Levine, A. (1980). *When dreams and heroes died*. San Francisco: Jossey-Bass.

Levine, A. (1994). Guerilla education in residential life. In C. Schroeder & P. Mable (Eds.), *Realizing the educational potential of residence halls* (pp. 93–106). San Francisco: Jossey-Bass.

Levine, A. (1997). Higher education becomes a mature industry. *About Campus, 2*, 31–32.

Levine, A., & Cureton, J. S. (1998a). Student politics: The new localism. *Review of Higher Education, 21*, 137–150.

Levine, A., & Cureton, J. S. (1998b). *When hope and fear collide*. San Francisco: Jossey-Bass.

Levine, A., & Cureton, J. S. (1998c). What we know about today's college students. *About Campus, 3*, 4–9.

Levine, A., & Cureton, J. S. (1998d). Student politics: The new localism: *Review of Higher Education, 21*, 137–150.

Lewin, K. (1947, June). Frontiers in group dynamics: Concept, method, and reality in social science: Social equilibria and social change. *Human Relations, 1*, 5–41.

Lickona, T. (1976). *Moral development and behavior: Theory, research, and social issues*. New York: Holt, Reinhart, and Winston.

Light, R. J. (1992). *The Harvard assessment seminars: Explorations with students and faculty about teaching, learning, and student life*. Cambridge, MA: Harvard University Graduate School of Education and Kennedy School of Government.

Light, R. J., Singer, J. D., & Willett, J. B. (1990). *By design: Planning research in higher education*. Cambridge, MA: Harvard University Press.

Lincoln, Y. S., & Guba, E. G. (1985). *Naturalistic inquiry*. Beverly Hills, CA: Sage.

Lippit, G., Langseth, P., & Mossop. J. (1985). *Implementing organizational change: A practical guide to managing change efforts*. San Francisco: Jossey-Bass.

Lloyd-Jones, E. M., & Smith, M. R. (1938). *A student personnel program for higher education*. New York: McGraw Hill.

London, H. B. (1996). How college affects first-generation students. *About Campus, 1*, 9–13.

Love, P. G. (1995). Interpretive frameworks: A qualitative analysis of individual sense-making in a department of residence life. *Journal of College Student Development, 36*, 234–241.

Love, P. G., Jacobs, B. A., Poschini, V. J., Hardy, C. M., & Kuh, G. D. (1993). Student culture. In G. D. Kuh (Ed.), *Cultural perspectives in student affairs work* (pp. 59–80). Washington, DC: American College Personnel Association.

Lovett, C. (1994). Assessment, CQI, and faculty culture. In AAHE Continuous Quality Improvement Project (Ed.), *CQI 101: A first reader for higher education* (pp. 143–152). Washington, DC: American Association for Higher Education.

Lund, J. (1995). *High expectations or high hopes? Using high expectations as an indicator for learning.* Unpublished manuscript, Indiana University at Bloomington.

Lyons, J. W. (1993). The importance of institutional mission. In M. J. Barr & Associates (Eds.), *The handbook of student affairs administration* (pp. 3–15). San Francisco: Jossey-Bass.

Magolda, P. M. (1997, May-June). Life as I don't know it. *About Campus, 2,* 16–22.

Malaney, G. D. (1993). A comprehensive student affairs research office. *NASPA Journal, 30,* 182–189.

Malaney, G. D., & Weitzer, W. H. (1993). Research on students: A framework of methods based on cost and expertise. *NASPA Journal, 30,* 126–137.

Manning, K., & Coleman-Boatwright, P. (1991). Student affairs initiatives toward a multicultural university. *Journal of College Student Development, 32,* 367–374.

Marchese, T. J. (1997). The new conversations about learning: Insights from neuroscience and anthropology, cognitive science, and workplace studies. In B. Cambridge (Ed.), *Assessing impact: Evidence and action* (pp. 79–95). Washington, DC: American Association for Higher Education.

Marchese, T. (1998). Not-so-distant competitors: How new providers are remaking the postsecondary marketplace. *AAHE Bulletin, 59*(9), 3–11.

Matthews, A. (1997). *Bright college years: Inside the American campus today.* New York: Simon & Schuster.

Mattox, B. A. (1975). *Getting it together: Dilemmas for the classroom.* San Diego: Pennant Press.

McMurtry, L. (1991). *Lonesome dove.* New York: Simon and Schuster.

Miami University Department of Communications. (1991). *Interactive video multicultural awareness information brochure.* Oxford, OH: Author.

Miami University Office of Residence Life and New Student Programs. (1997). *The 1997 Miami University Resident Assistant Institute.* Oxford, OH: Author.

Minor, F. D. (1997, March/April). Bringing it home: Integrating classroom and residential experiences. *About Campus, 2,* 21–22.

Mintz, S. D., & Hesser, G. W. (1996). Principles of good practice in service learning. In B. Jacoby & Associates (Eds.), *Service learning in higher education: Concepts and practices* (pp. 26–52). San Francisco: Jossey-Bass.

Moneta, L. (1997). The integration of technology with the management of student services. In C. M. Engstrom & K. W. Kruger (Eds.), *Using technology to promote student learning: Opportunities for today and tomorrow* (pp. 5–16). San Francisco: Jossey-Bass.

Morrill, R. L. (1980). *Teaching values in college.* San Francisco: Jossey-Bass.

Motley, E. L. and Corts, T. E. (1996). Student government: Friend or foe? *About Campus, 1*(4), 28–30.

Napoli, A. R., & Wortman, P. M. (in press). Psychosocial factors related to retention and early departure of two-year community college students. *Research in Higher Education.*

National Association of State Universities and Land-Grant Colleges. (1997). *Returning to our roots: The student experience.* Washington, DC: Author.

National Association of Student Personnel Administrators. (1987). *A perspective on student affairs.* Washington, DC: Author.

National Center for Education Statistics (1994). *The condition of education.* Washington, DC: United States Department of Education.

National Center for Higher Education Management Systems. (1994). *A preliminary study of the feasibility and utility for national policy of instructional "good practice" indicators in undergraduate education.* Washington, D.C.: U.S. Department of Education, Office of Educational Research and Improvement.

National Commission on the Cost of Higher Education. (1998, January). *Straight talk about college costs and prices.* Washington, DC: Author.

National Commission on Excellence in Education. (1983). *A nation at risk.* Washington, DC: U.S. Department of Education.

Newton, F. B. (1998). The stressed student—how can we help? *About Campus, 3,* 4–10.

Olsen, D. (1997). *Preliminary look at students' expectations of IU Bloomington: How well do their expectations fit ours?* Bloomington: Indiana University Office of Academic Affairs.

Pace, C. R. (1990). *College Student Experiences Questionnaire* (3rd ed.). Bloomington, IN: Indiana University, School of Education, Center for Postsecondary Research and Planning.

Palmer, P. J. (1987, September/October). Community, conflict, and ways of knowing. *Change, 19,* 20–25.

Palmer, P. J. (1990, January/February). Good teaching: A matter of living the mystery. *Change, 22,* 11–16.

Parks, S. (1990). *The critical years: The young adult's search for meaning, faith, and commitment.* New York: Harper and Row.

Pascarella, E. T. (1997, January/February). It's time we started paying attention to community college students. *About Campus, 1,* 14–17.

Pascarella, E. T., Bohr, L., Nora, A., & Terenzini, P. T. (1995a). Cognitive effects of two-year and four-year colleges: New evidence. *Educational Evaluation and Policy Analysis, 17*(1), 83–96.

Pascarella, E. T., Bohr, L., Nora, A., & Terenzini, P. T. (1995b). Intercollegiate athletic participation and freshman year cognitive outcomes. *Journal of Higher Education, 66*, 369–387.

Pascarella, E. T., Edison, M., Nora, A., Hagedorn, L., & Braxton, J. (1995). *Effects of teacher organization/preparation and teacher skill/clarity on general cognitive skills in college.* Paper presented at the annual meeting of the American Educational Research Association, San Francisco.

Pascarella, E. T., Edison, M., Nora, A., Hagedorn, L. S., & Terenzini, P. T. (1996). Influences on students' openness to diversity and challenge in the first year of college. *Journal of Higher Education, 67*, 174–195.

Pascarella, E. T., Edison, M., Nora, A., Hagedorn, L. S., & Terenzini, P. T. (1998). Does work inhibit cognitive development during the first year of college? *Journal of Educational Evaluation and Policy Analysis.*

Pascarella, E. T., Edison, M., Whitt, E. J., Nora, A., Hagedorn, L. S., & Terenzini, P. T. (1996). Cognitive effects of Greek affiliation during the first year of college. *NASPA Journal, 33*, 242–257.

Pascarella, E. T., & Terenzini, P. T. (1991). *How college affects students.* San Francisco: Jossey-Bass.

Pascarella, E. T., & Terenzini, P. T. (1998). Studying college students in the 21st century: Meeting new challenges. *Review of Higher Education, 21*, 151–165.

Pascarella, E. T., Whitt, E. J., Edison, M. I., Nora, A., Hagedorn, L. S., Yeager, P. M., & Terenzini, P. T. (1997). Women's perceptions of a "chilly climate" and their cognitive outcomes during the first year of college. *Journal of College Student Development, 38*, 109–124.

Pascarella, E. T., Whitt, E. J., Nora, A., Edison, M., Hagedorn, L. S., & Terenzini, P. T. (1996). What have we learned from the first year of the National Study of Student Learning? *Journal of College Student Development, 37*, 182–192.

Pedersen, P. (1988). *Handbook for developing multicultural awareness.* Alexandria, VA: American Association of Counseling and Development.

Perry, W. (1970). *Forms of intellectual and ethical development during the college years.* New York: Holt, Reinhart, and Winston.

Pfeiffer, J. W., & Jones, J. E. (Eds.). (1983). *The 1983 annual handbook for group facilitators.* LaJolla, CA: University Associates Publishers.

Pike, G. A. (1996, Fall). *A student success story: Freshman interest groups at the University of Missouri, Columbia* (MU Student Life Studies Abstracts No.1). Unpublished report.

Pike, G., Schroeder, C., & Berry, T. (1997). Enhancing the educational impact of residence halls: The relationship between residential learning communities and first-year college experiences. *Journal of College Student Development*, *38*, 609–621.

Piper, T. D. (1996, November). The community standards model: A method to enhance student learning and development. *Association of College and University Housing Officers-International Talking Stick*, 14–15.

Piper, T. D. (1997, July/August). Empowering students to create community standards. *About Campus*, *2*, 22–24.

Piper, T. R., Gentile, M. C., & Parks, S. D. (1993). *Can ethics be taught?* Boston: Harvard Business School.

Pruitt, D. A. (1996, July/August). The Carolinian's creed. *About Campus*, *1*, 27–30.

Ravitch, D. (1996, October 7). Why do Catholic schools succeed? *Forces*, 81.

Reisser, L. (1993). *Teamwork assessment*. Unpublished manuscript.

Reisser, L. (1996, October). *The keys to community*. Paper presented at the Northwest College Personnel Association, Spokane, WA.

Rendon, L. I. (1996). Life on the border. *About Campus*, *1*, 14–20.

Rendon, L. I. (1998). Helping nontraditional students be successful in college. *About Campus*, *3*, 2–3.

Resnikoff, A., & Jennings, J. S. (1982). The view from within: Perspectives from the intensive case study. In J. M. Whiteley et al. (Eds.), *Character development in college students* (Vol. 1, pp. 195–222). Schenectady, NY: Character Research Press.

Rest, J. R. (1975). Longitudinal study of the defining issues test: A strategy for analyzing developmental change. *Developmental Psychology*, *11*, 738–748.

Rest, J. R. (1979). *Development in judging moral issues*. Minneapolis: University of Minnesota Press.

Rhoads, R. A. (1994). *Coming out in college: The struggle for queer identity*. Westport, CT: Bergin & Garvey.

Rhoads, R. A. (1995a). Learning from the coming-out experiences of college males. *Journal of College Student Development*, *36*, 67–74.

Rhoads, R. A. (1995b). Whales tales, dog piles, and beer goggles: An ethnographic case study of fraternity life. *Anthropology and Education Quarterly*, *26*, 306–323.

Rhoads, R. A., & Black, M. A. (1995). Student affairs practitioners as transformative educators: Advancing a critical cultural perspective. *Journal of College Student Development*, *36*, 413–421.

RiCharde, R. S., Olney, C. A., & Erwin, T. D. (1993). Cognitive and affective measures of student development. In T. W. Banta & Associates (Eds.), *Making a difference: Outcomes of a decade of assessment in higher education* (pp. 179–195). San Francisco: Jossey-Bass.

Roebuck, J., & Murty, K. S. (1993). *Historically Black colleges and universities: Their place in American higher education*. New York: Praeger.

Rogers, J. L. (1996). Leadership. In S. R. Komives & D. B. Woodard, Jr. (Eds.), *Student services: A handbook for the profession* (pp. 299–319). San Francisco: Jossey-Bass.

Romano, C. K. (1996). A qualitative study of women student leaders. *Journal of College Student Development, 37*(6), 676–683.

Roper, L. D. (1996). Teaching and training. In S. R. Komives & D. B. Woodard, Jr. (Eds.), *Student services: A handbook for the profession* (pp. 320–334). San Francisco: Jossey-Bass.

Rosenthal, R. (1993). Interpersonal expectations: Some antecedents and some consequences. In P. D. Blanck (Ed.), *Interpersonal expectations: Theory, research, and applications* (pp. 3–24). Cambridge, UK: Cambridge University Press.

Rosenthal, R., & Jacobson, L. (1968). *Pygmalion in the classroom: Teacher expectation and pupils' intellectual development*. New York: Holt, Rinehart, & Winston.

Sandeen, A. (1991). *The chief student affairs officer*. San Francisco: Jossey-Bass.

Sax, L. J., Astin, A. W., Arredondo, M., & Korn, W. S. (1996). *The American college teacher: National norms for the 1995–96 HERI faculty survey*. Los Angeles: University of California, Los Angeles, Higher Education Research Institute.

Sax, L. J., Astin, A. W., Korn, W. S., & Mahoney, K. M. (1995). *The American college freshman*. Los Angeles: University of California, Higher Education Research Institute.

Schein, E. H. (1992). *Organizational culture and leadership* (2nd ed.). San Francisco: Jossey-Bass.

Schmidt, W. H., & Finnegan, J. P. (1992). *The race without a finish line*. San Francisco, CA: Jossey-Bass.

Schroeder, C. C. (1994). Developing learning communities. In C. C. Schroeder & P. Mable (Eds.), *Realizing the educational potential of residence halls* (pp. 165–189). San Francisco: Jossey-Bass.

Schroeder, C. C., & Hurst, J. C. (1996). Designing learning environments that integrate curricular and cocurricular experiences. *Journal of College Student Development, 37*, 174–181.

Schroeder, C. C., Nicholls, G. E., & Kuh, G. D. (1983). Exploring the rain forest: Testing assumptions and taking risks. In G. D. Kuh (Ed.), *Understanding student affairs organizations* (New Directions for Student Services No. 23, pp. 51–66). San Francisco: Jossey-Bass.

Selman, R. (1976). A developmental approach to interpersonal and moral awareness in young children: Some theoretical and educational implications of levels of social perspective-taking. In J. R. Meyer, B. Burnham, & J. Cholvat (Eds.), *Values education* (pp. 127–139). Waterloo, Ontario: Wilfred Laurier University Press.

Senge, P. M. (1990a). *The fifth discipline: The art and practice of the learning organization.* New York: Doubleday.

Senge, P. M. (1990b). The leader's new work: Building learning organizations. *Sloan Management Review, 32*(1), 7–23.

Seven Principles Resource Center. (1989). *Faculty inventory: Principles for good practice in undergraduate education.* Winona, MN: Winona State University.

Seven Principles Resource Center. (1989). Student inventory: Principles for good practice in undergraduate education. Winona, MN: Winona State University.

Seymour, D. (1995). *Once upon a campus: Lessons for improving quality and productivity in higher education.* Phoenix, AZ: American Council on Education.

Shattuck, R. (1997, July 18). From school to college: We must end the conspiracy to lower standards. *Chronicle of Higher Education*, p. B7.

Shavlik, D. L., Touchton, J. G., & Pearson, C. S. (1989). The new agenda of women for higher education. In C. S. Pearson, D. L. Shavlik, & J. G. Touchton (Eds.), *Educating the majority: Women challenge tradition in higher education*, pp. 441–458. New York: ACE-MacMillan.

Sheehan, R. (1996, September 29). Campus courts on trial. *The Sunday News and Observer*, pp. 1A, 20A.

Shor, I. (1992). *Empowering education: Critical teaching for social change.* Chicago, IL: University of Chicago Press.

Snyder, M., & Swann, W. B., Jr. (1978). Hypothesis-testing processes in social interaction. Journal of Personality and Social Psychology, 36, *1202–1212.*

Sorcinelli, M. D. (1991). Research findings on the seven principles. In A. W. Chickering & Z. F. Gamson (Eds.), *Applying the seven principles for good practice in undergraduate education* (New Directions for Teaching and Learning No. 47, pp. 13–25). San Francisco: Jossey-Bass.

Stage, F. K. (1992). The case for flexibility in research and assessment of college students. In F. K. Stage (Ed.), *Diverse methods for research and assessment of college students* (pp. 1–12). Alexandria, VA: American College Personnel Association.

Stein, W. J. (1992). *Tribally controlled colleges: Making good medicine*. New York: Lang.

Stimpson, R. (1993). Selecting and training competent staff. In M. J. Barr & Associates (Eds.), *The handbook of student affairs administration* (pp. 135–151). San Francisco: Jossey-Bass.

Stimpson, R. (1994). Creating a context for educational success. In C. Schroeder & P. Mable (Eds.), *Realizing the educational potential of residence halls* (pp. 53–69). San Francisco: Jossey-Bass.

Stombler, M., & Martin, P. Y. (1994). Bringing women in, keeping women down: Fraternity "little sister" organizations. *Journal of Contemporary Ethnography, 23,* 150–184.

Strange, C. C. (1996). Dynamics of campus environments. In S. R. Komives & D. B. Woodward, Jr. (Ed.), *Student services: A handbook for the profession* (3rd ed., pp. 244–268). San Francisco: Jossey-Bass.

Study Group on Conditions of Excellence in Higher Education. (1984). *Involvement in learning: Realizing the potential of American higher education*. Washington, DC: National Institute of Education.

Suffolk County Community College (Ammerman Campus). (1995, December). *Role and scope statement*. Selden, NY: Author.

Swidler, A. (1997, May 16). To revitalize community life, we must first strengthen our national institutions. *Chronicle of Higher Education*, pp. B4–B6.

Talbot, D. M. (1996). Multiculturalism. In Komives, S. R. & Woodward, D. B., Jr. (Eds.), *Student services: A handbook for the profession* (3rd ed., pp. 380–396). San Francisco: Jossey-Bass.

Terenzini, P. T. (1989). Assessment with open eyes: Pitfalls in studying student outcomes. *Journal of Higher Education, 60,* 644–664.

Terenzini, P. T., & Pascarella, E. T. (1994, January/February). Living with myths: Undergraduate education in America. *Change, 26,* 28–32.

Terenzini, P. T., Pascarella, E. T., & Blimling, G. S. (1996). Students' out-of-class experiences and their influence on learning and cognitive development: A literature review. *Journal of College Student Development, 37,* 149–162.

Terenzini, P. T., Springer, L., Pascarella, E. T., & Nora, A. (1995a). Influences affecting the development of students' critical thinking skills. *Research in Higher Education, 36,* 23–39.

Terenzini, P. T., Springer, L., Pascarella, E. T., & Nora, A. (1995b). Academic and out-of-class influences on students' intellectual orientations. *Review of Higher Education, 19*(2), 23–44.

Tinto, V. (1993). *Leaving college: Rethinking the causes and cures of student attrition* (2nd ed.). Chicago: University of Chicago Press.

Tinto, V. (1997, January/February). Universities as learning organizations. *About Campus, 1,* 2–3.

Upcraft, M. L., & Schuh, J. H. (1996). *Assessment in student affairs.* San Francisco: Jossey-Bass.

Wahbe, M. (1990, July). *Current issues in human services: The Satir model.* A workshop sponsored by Western Washington University and the Northwest Satir Institute, Bellingham, WA.

Walton, M. (1986). *The Deming management method.* New York: Dodd, Mead & Company.

Warren, R. G. (1997, March/April). Engaging students in active learning. *About Campus, 2,* 16–20.

Weick, K. E. (1983). Contradictions in a community of scholars: The cohesion/accuracy tradeoff. *Review of Higher Education, 20,* 23–33.

Weick, K. E. (1995). *Sense-making in organizations.* Thousand Oaks, CA: Sage.

Weingartner, R. H. (1994, Winter). Between cup and lip: Reconceptualizing education as students learning. *Educational Record, 75,* 13–19.

Weitzer, W. H., & Malaney, G. D. (1991). Of puzzles and pieces: Organizing and directing a campus-based research agenda. In K. J. Beeler & D. E. Hunter (Eds.), *Puzzles and pieces in wonderland: The promise and practice of student affairs research* (pp. 35–54). Washington, DC: National Association of Student Personnel Administrators.

Western Cooperative for Educational Communications. (1996, March/April). Principles of good practice for electronically offered academic degree and certificate programs. *Change, 28,* 40.

Whitehead, A. N. (1929). *The aims of education and other essays.* New York: Free Press.

Whitt, E. J. (1991). Artful science: A primer on qualitative research methods. *Journal of College Student Development, 32,* 406–415.

Whitt, E. J. (1994a). Encouraging adult learner involvement. *NASPA Journal, 31,* 309–318.

Whitt, E. J. (1994b). I can be anything! Student leadership in three women's colleges. *Journal of College Student Development, 35,* 198–207.

Whitt, E. J. (1996a, September/October). Some propositions worth debating. *About Campus, 1,* 31–32.

Whitt, E. J. (1996b). Assessing student cultures. In J. H. Schuh & M. L. Upcraft

(Eds.), *Assessment in student affairs* (pp. 189–216). San Francisco: Jossey-Bass.

Whitt, E. J., & Associates (1998). *Student learning as student affairs work.* Washington, DC: National Association of Student Personnel Administrators.

Whitt, E. J., Edison, M. I., Pascarella, E. T., Nora, A., & Terenzini, P. T. (1997). Interactions with peers and objective and self-reported cognitive outcomes across three years of college. *Journal of College Student Development.*

Wilder, C., Sherrier, J., & Berry, W. (1991). *Learning activity proposal for PDA 101 (Pluralism and Diversity in America).* Suffern, NY: Rockland Community College, Office of Instructional and Community Services.

Williams, L. B. (1997, May/June). Telling tales in school. *About Campus, 2,* 2–3.

Wilson R. (1996). Educating for diversity. *About Campus, 2*(5), 2–3.

Wingspread Group on Higher Education. (1993a). *An American imperative: Higher expectations for higher education.* Racine, WI: The Johnson Foundation.

Wingspread Group on Higher Education. (1993b). An open letter to those concerned about the American future. In the Wingspread Group on Higher Education (Ed.), *An American imperative: Higher expectations for higher education.* Racine, WI: The Johnson Foundation.

Young, R. B. (1996). Guiding values and philosophy. In S. R. Komives and D. B. Woodward, Jr. (Eds.), *Student services: A handbook for the profession* (pp. 83–105). San Francisco: Jossey-Bass.

Index